TIME
FOR KIDS

That's
Strange
BUT TRUE!

The World's Most Astonishing
Facts & Records

TIME FOR KIDS

That's Strange BUT TRUE!

TIME FOR KIDS

Managing Editor, TIME For Kids: Nellie Gonzalez Cutler
Editor, Time Learning Ventures: Jonathan Rosenbloom

Book Packager: R studio T, New York City
Art Direction/Design: Raúl Rodriguez and Rebecca Tachna
Writer: Lora Myers
Photo Researchers: Miriam Budnick, Elizabeth Vezzulla
Designer: Ames Montgomery
Photographer: Craig Deutsch
Copy Editor: Krissy Roleke
Image Editor: John Gibson
Fact-Checkers: Luis Pereyra, Audrey Whitley
Acknowledgments: Talia Aisha Baxter and Erika Baxter, Jenna and Lauren Bell, Cheri and Joe Bell, Virigina Provost at Terrafugia Inc., Dan Cameron at Queensland Art Gallery, Fred Selby at Watercar.com, Maria Livia Breccia at OMA.com, Frank Glaw, Eric Watts at Trektrak.com, John Pilley and Chaser

TIME HOME ENTERTAINMENT

Publisher: Richard Fraiman
Vice President, Business Development & Strategy: Steven Sandonato
Executive Director, Marketing Services: Carol Pittard
Executive Director, Retail & Special Sales: Tom Mifsud
Executive Publishing Director: Joy Butts
Director, Bookazine Development & Marketing: Laura Adam
Finance Director: Glenn Buonocore
Associate Publishing Director: Megan Pearlman
Assistant General Counsel: Helen Wan
Assistant Director, Special Sales: Ilene Schreider
Senior Book Production Manager: Susan Chodakiewicz
Design & Prepress Manager: Anne-Michelle Gallero
Brand Manager: Jonathan White
Associate Prepress Manager: Alex Voznesenskiy
Assistant Brand Manager: Stephanie Braga

Editorial Director: Stephen Koepp
Editorial Operations Director: Michael Q. Bullerdick

Special thanks to: Christine Austin, Jeremy Biloon, Alex Borinstein, Jim Childs, Rose Cirrincione, Lauren Hall Clark, Jacqueline Fitzgerald, Christine Font, Suzanne Janso, Raphael Joa, David Kahn, Jeffrey Kaji, Mona Li, Robert Marasco, Kimberly Marshall, Amy Migliaccio, Nina Mistry, Richard Prue, Myles Ringel, Dave Rozzelle, Sasha Shapiro, Soren Shapiro, Adriana Tierno, Time Imaging, Vanessa Wu

For information on TIME For Kids magazine for the classroom or home, go to www.tfkclassroom.com or call 1-800-777-8600.

For subscriptions to Sports Illustrated Kids, go to www.sikids.com or call 1-800-889-6007.

Published by TIME For Kids Books
Time Inc.
1271 Avenue of the Americas
New York, New York 10020

ISBN 10: 1-60320-199-8
ISBN 13: 978-1-60320-199-5
Library of Congress No.: 2011929052

"TIME For Kids" is a trademark of Time Inc.

We welcome your comments and suggestions about TIME For Kids Books. Please write to us at:
TIME For Kids Books
Attention: Book Editors
P.O. Box 11016
Des Moines, IA 50336-1016

If you would like to order any of our hardcover Collector's Edition books, please call us at 1-800-327-6388 (Monday through Friday, 7:00 a.m.– 8:00 p.m., or Saturday, 7:00 a.m.– 6:00 p.m., Central Time).

1 TLF 12

Contents

26

44

57

79

140

152

160

167

It's a STRANGE BUT TRUE World!

Science-fiction fans love the weirdness of alien worlds. But take a good look around you. The truth is: Some of the most wondrously strange sights, sounds, tastes, inventions, and people in the universe are right here at home—and lurking between the pages of this book!

LOCATION:
London, England
Who still believes the Earth is flat? You'll be amazed by SBT Ideas.

LOCATION:
Amarillo, Texas
What makes tourists flock to Cadillac Ranch? Travel to SBT Sites and Sights.

LOCATION:
North Atlantic U.S. coast
What weather-loving artist turns hurricanes into sculptures? Come admire SBT Art.

LOCATION: Mexico City, Mexico
Can humans live in a nautilus shell? Take a tour of SBT Buildings.

LOCATION:
Buñol, Spain
Why do festivalgoers throw rotten tomatoes? Plunge into SBT Sports and Contests.

LOCATION:
Amazon area
Is this where the Lost City of Gold can be found? Be adventurous with SBT Quests.

W E
N
S

LOCATION: Adriatic Sea
Which creature can live for years without eating? All is revealed in SBT Animals and Plants.

LOCATION: Japan
How can cat ears help people express emotions? SBT Science and Technology explains.

LOCATION: Somewhere in Africa and Southeast Asia
Where do real fakirs hang out? Nobody fakes it in SBT Body Feats.

LOCATION: Uganda
What happens when you combine a drum and a computer? SBT Inventions tells the story.

LOCATION: Goulburn, Australia
Who is the real Rambo? Size up SBT Size.

CHAPTER 1

Animals and Plants

A slime-spewing fish?
A two-headed turtle?
A plant that plays dead?
These are just a few of the
strange but absolutely,
positively true creatures
and organisms on our
planet…and in this book!

Strange

A psychedelic frog…

In This Chapter

- Animals with Aptitude
- Bionic Critters
- Astounding Plants

  And Much More!

Stranger

A tortoise on wheels…

Strangest

A dog with a huge vocabulary!

Hide-and-Seek

Every year, hundreds of animal species disappear. But sometimes, scientists get a happy surprise. They come across an animal that was thought to be extinct but is alive and well.

Return of the Bornean Rainbow Toad

The last time anybody saw this poisonous amphibian with the multicolor, pebbly back was in 1924. Then, in 2011, a group of scientists in Malaysia was looking for species that people thought were extinct. To their surprise, they spotted three rainbow toads—a baby and two adults. The scientists took photos to let the world know that these creatures are still on the planet.

Ssssurprise Sssssnake

For 100 years, the only Madagascar blind snakes that herpetologists (scientists who study amphibians and reptiles) got to see were two dead specimens in a museum. But on a recent expedition to Madagascar, an island off the southeastern coast of Africa, the snake seekers spotted one. It was bright pink and as thin as a pencil. It was a lucky find, because this species of snake, which has poor vision and is super-sensitive to light, tends to hide under piles of sand or layers of rocks.

Most Wanted Species

Here are five animals that are in danger of dying out. The main reasons are habitat loss and illegal hunting.

1. Tiger Its bones are used in traditional Chinese medicines, and its skin is sold as rugs.

2. Napoleon wrasse The big-lipped, bright blue fish are sold in certain restaurants for hundreds of dollars a portion.

3. Great white shark Its jaws, teeth, fins, and hide fetch high prices worldwide.

4. Pig-nosed turtle These freshwater turtles from Papua New Guinea are in great demand as pets.

5. Yellow-crested cockatoo Stolen from the jungles of Indonesia, the cockatoos are sold as pets worldwide.

Weird Fish

You might think there's something fishy about these creatures, but strange as they may seem, they're all for real. And what they can do may surprise you.

Eggs-cellent!

He looks fierce, but this male yellow-striped cardinalfish is doing delicate work. He is carrying a load of eggs that were released in the water by a female cardinalfish. Dad will keep the eggs safe in his mouth for about a week. Then he'll spit out the larvae when they hatch.

Get Slimed

You don't want to run into hagfish in the Pacific Ocean, where they lurk, often under rocks. Here's why: When threatened, a hagfish defends itself by spewing slime from its many pores and coating its enemy in a giant blob of gunk.

Oh, Give Me an Olm

The **olm** is an amphibian that never leaves the water. It is blind—but has excellent hearing and smell—and can live to be 100 years old. The strangest thing about it is that it can survive for 10 years without eating. It's found in underwater caves deep in the Adriatic Sea.

The Electric Freshwater Elephant

Where else would you find an **elephant fish** but in the freshwaters of Africa? Like their namesakes, they have long, trunklike noses and are considered highly intelligent. Scientists are fascinated by these strange fish, because they generate electric fields that appear to help other fish find their way through murky water.

Happy Endings

There are about 75 million dogs and 85 million cats owned by pet lovers in the United States, not to mention tens of millions of other types of pets, from parrots to pythons. You can bet that a huge number of them one day or another will get lost—and it will take a lot of luck for their owners to find them again.

Swept Away

When a terrible earthquake and tsunami (soo-*na*-mee) struck Japan in 2011, entire cities were destroyed and thousands of people were killed. Amid the destruction, a mixed-breed dog named **Ban** was washed out to sea. But the plucky dog clung to pieces of debris and floated on the waves without food or water for three weeks until rescuers found him. Luckily, Ban's owner spotted him in a story on the nightly news—and they were quickly and happily reunited.

A Pooch on Facebook

When a Florida woman found a lost Lhasa apso outside her home in Tamarac, Florida, she checked the little dog's microchip for clues. The chip showed the dog's name—Topaz—and the names of her owners. But the owners were nowhere to be found in Florida. So the woman searched Facebook for people of the same name and posted a note about Topaz. She got a reply from the owners, who had had to give up their pet to a family in Tampa four years earlier. No one knows how Topaz traveled 200 miles from Tampa to Tamarac. But thanks to Facebook, she was reunited with her BFFs!

FLORIDA

Tampa

Tamarac

Willow's Travels

It's a long, long way from Colorado to New York. That didn't stop Willow, a calico cat, from making it to the streets of the Big Apple—1,800 miles from her Rocky Mountain family. More than five years after Willow disappeared, she was taken in by New York City's animal rescue and shelter system. Thanks to her microchip, the wandering Willow was returned to her excited owners, who wondered what kind of life she led while she had been away. But Willow's not talking!

New York

Colorado

Animal Aptitude

Humans are learning more about the workings of animals' minds. It turns out that many members of the animal kingdom are smarter than people once thought.

Where *did* I put Mr. Potato Head?

Get This Dog a Dictionary

Most dogs understand a dozen or so words, but **Chaser**, a female border collie, knows more than 1,000 words. Chaser's owner taught her to fetch specific objects by name from a huge pile of 800 stuffed animals, 116 balls, and 26 Frisbees. For example, if Chaser's owner says, "Fetch Mr. Potato Head!" the dog will dig into the pile and come up with that very item.

Abuzz About Math

A bee may not be able to solve for *x*, but the busy insect can solve a complex math problem. Researchers observed that when bees have to figure out the shortest routes from one flower to another, they do it instantly. In fact, they do it faster than a supercomputer, which might take several days to do all possible calculations.

Have we met?

Pigeon Power

Lots of people love to feed pigeons. If you're one of the many who don't, be careful. It's possible the bird will remember your face! Two researchers made that discovery when they conducted a simple experiment on a street in Paris, France. They both dressed in the same white lab coats and both put out food for the birds. According to plan, one researcher let the pigeons eat peacefully while the other chased them away. The next few times the researchers fed the birds, the humans wore different clothing. The two researchers left the birds alone. But the pigeons seemed to recognize the face of the person who had first chased them away—and stayed clear.

TFK TOP 5
Smartest Animals

ANIMALS	WHAT THEY CAN DO
1. Chimpanzees	Use tools, solve problems, communicate with humans
2. Dolphins	Use sophisticated language, teach their young, learn human commands
3. Orangutans	Communicates with hand gestures, teach their young
4. Elephants	Use tools, learn human commands
5. Crows	Use tools, use tricks to get what they want

Bionic Critters

If a starfish loses an arm, it can grow it back again. Many insects and amphibians can naturally replace lost legs or tails. But what about the majority of animals that can't regenerate body parts when they are injured? It's up to humans to help out!

Two-Wheeled Tortoise

After its leg was bitten off by a hungry rat, Tuly, a tortoise in England, was near death. Her owners rushed her to the pet hospital for a just-in-time operation. But soon afterward, the vets noticed that when Tuly moved about, she was scraping the underside of her shell, wearing it away. So, the doctors fitted Tuly with the wheels from a child's toy car—and now Tuly can safely tool around.

Cat's Paws– Back in Service

Bionic limbs are no longer just for people! A veterinary surgeon in England implanted two artificial rear feet on a cat named Oscar after he had been hurt by a piece of machinery. Four months later, Oscar was standing tall on his two unusual metal paws. And there's a bonus: Prosthetics—artificial limbs—designed for animals are teaching doctors new ways to help injured human patients.

Midnite Trots Again

Midnite, a four-year-old miniature horse, arrived at Ranch Hand Rescue, a charity ranch, in Texas, that takes care of abused or rescued farm animals. He was underweight and in bad shape. Because he had been born missing a hoof and part of his lower leg, he couldn't run. Veterinarians thought they would have to remove his lower leg.

Then Bob Williams, the head of Ranch Hand Rescue, had an idea. Why couldn't Midnite be fitted with an artificial limb, just like a human can? ProsthetiCare, a company in Fort Worth, Texas, that makes artificial limbs, thought that was a great idea. The company agreed to make and donate Midnite's new leg and hoof. It was the first of its kind.

After his second fitting, Midnite—who before had struggled just to get on his feet—began to run around the ranch. Everyone who watched him was thrilled. Midnite became a healthy and mobile horse. "It's amazing to see the difference in him," Williams told TFK.

Caring for Midnite is a big job, but the ranch staff enjoys doing it. They remove the limb three times a day to clean it and to massage Midnite's leg. They also limit his movement so he doesn't get hurt. But Midnite is happiest when he's a four-legged horse again. "You put his prosthetic on, and he perks right up," Williams says, smiling.

Midnite's new limb has an artificial hoof. The limb is attached with Velcro straps. It's the first of its kind.

Welcome, Strangers!

Every year, botanists and biologists discover strange species of plants and animals. Between 1990 and 2010, 1,300 organisms were identified and added to the list. Here are four newly found creatures. Scientists will study these and the other 1,296 newcomers in the hope of learning more about the way our ecosystems work.

Nosy Bat

This little bat, from the mountains of Papua New Guinea, in the South Pacific Ocean, had already been spotted by scientists—but never given a name. Doesn't **tube-nosed fruit bat** seem just about right? Or, you may call it the Yoda bat, because it looks something like the Jedi Master in *Star Wars*. What do fruit bats live on? Fruit and flower nectar.

Up a Tree

Looking like a cross between a skunk and a porcupine, the **chinchilla tree rat** was discovered in southeastern Peru. It's about the size of a house cat, and has sharp claws—the better to climb trees with. Zoologists think this rodent is related to chinchilla rats found in the tombs of ancient Incans who may have kept them as pets or for food.

Ancient Arachnid

If this spider looks like it's encrusted with age, that's because it belongs to a group of arachnids that have been around for over 300 million years. No wonder it's nicknamed the **dinospider.** Found in Central and South America and West Africa, this newly discovered species eats termites and larvae, and helps recycle organic materials back into the ground.

BTW

Conservation International (CI) is one organization behind the discovery of new plants and animals. CI sends "ecological SWAT teams"—groups of field biologists—to search for rare and previously unknown species around the world.

Far-Out Salamander

The weirdest thing about the **E.T. salamander,** discovered by scientists in the rain forests of southern Ecuador, is that it has no lungs. Instead, it breathes through its skin. It also has webbed feet that enable it to climb up to the treetops of its tropical home.

Peculiar Plants

Gardeners and botanists, scientists who study plants, know that every plant has special characteristics. Take a look at some of them.

Eat Your Fractal!

Math lovers love the Romanesco broccoli, a type of cauliflower, and not just because it's tasty. The plant grows in spiral patterns that are fractals, natural forms of Fibonacci numbers. Studying the way that the spirals repeat themselves at different scales might help raise your math scores!

Don't Play Ball

How strange is this—a South African cactus that would look at home in a catcher's mitt! No wonder it's nicknamed the baseball plant. But hands off! So many people have been collecting samples from the wild that the baseball plant is now a protected species.

Do You Smell Something?

If a plant needs to attract dung beetles to pollinate it, it helps if the plant smells like dung. That's the aroma of *Hydnora africana*, a parasitic plant that looks something like a snake's open jaws. Found in the deserts of southern Africa, this bizarre plant has evolved its smell so that dung beetles will hang out inside its flower long enough to deposit or collect pollen. Eventually, the beetles crawl out and move on to the next stinky *Hydnora* and repeat the process.

Playing Dead

Mimosa pudica (mee-*mo*-sa *poo*-dee-ka) is its Latin name; touch-me-not is its nickname. That's because this sensitive little flowering herb, native to Central and South America, plays dead when it feels threatened. If a predator brushes against it, or a human tries to touch it, each stem releases a chemical that causes the leaves to shrivel up. A few minutes later, when the plant senses the coast is clear, it comes back to life.

The touch-me-not's leaves are usually open . . .

. . . but when it's threatened, it curls its leaves and plays dead.

Seeing Double

Everybody knows how sad it is to lose a much-loved pet. But these days, the amazing technology of cloning can create a new animal that looks incredibly like the original.

Lancelot Returns

In 2009, when a Florida couple lost their Labrador retriever, Sir Lancelot, they were grief-stricken. They missed him so much that they decided to see if a genetically identical Lab could be cloned using frozen DNA that had been taken from Sir Lancelot six years earlier. A Korean biotech company did the job for $155,000, making the new pet, Sir Lancelot Encore, the first American puppy to be commercially cloned. Now the question is: Will he behave just like his ancestor—or will he develop his own personality?

Oh, Give Me a Clone

Pets cloned from the same animal aren't like identical twins. Missy Two and Mira are clones of a border collie–husky mix named Missy, who died in 2002. But Missy's clones don't look exactly alike, because they were born several months apart to different mother dogs. Still, their owner claims both animals get their intelligence and good nature from Missy's DNA.

Hello, Dolly

Meet Dolly, the sheep whose birth in Scotland in 1997 created a worldwide sensation. Dolly was the first mammal to be successfully cloned from the cell of another mammal. As one excited scientist put it: "You can almost divide science into two segments: Before Dolly and After Dolly.… We didn't think that cloning could be done at all." Since Dolly was born, cows, goats, pigs, rats, mice, rabbits, horses, mules, and other mammals have all been successfully cloned.

For Real? A STRANGE BUT TRUE GAME

Seeing is not necessarily believing in this supercomputer age. Photographers can create pictures of animals and plants that never existed in nature. Take a look at these photos. Are these animals fakes? The answers are at the bottom of page 27.

A. Two-Headed Horse

Is truth stranger than fiction? Or is this horse a fake?

B. Two-Headed Turtle

Is this a real
two-headed turtle?

C. Two-Headed Gray Crowned Crane

Does this bird really
have two heads?

D. Six-Legged Frog

Is this a real frog with six legs?

Answers: A. If you guessed this is a fake
photograph, you're right! B. Strange but True:
This turtle is for real. C. Nope. This is a picture
of two birds standing close together.
D. Believe it or not, this frog has six legs.

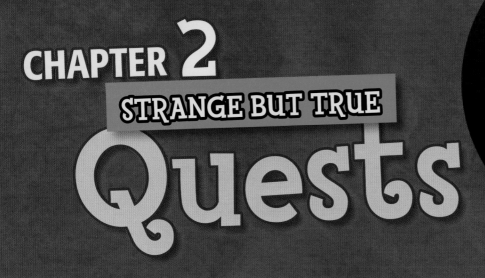

CHAPTER 2

Quests

Will 21st-century adventurers find Atlantis? Who will locate the famous lost gold mines of the American West? What forgotten riches await fearless deep-sea divers? Read on to experience some of the world's most daring quests for treasure and adventure.

In This Chapter

- Going for Gold
- Under the Waves
- Antarctic Adventures
  And Much More!

Strange

The search for golden treasure in Arizona's Superstition mountains…

Enters ice pack
(58°-40'S 18°W.)

1000 miles forced through icebergs

Stranger

**The hair-raising adventures
of explorer Ernest Shackleton
in Antarctica…**

Strangest

The tale of the Lost Continent of Mu

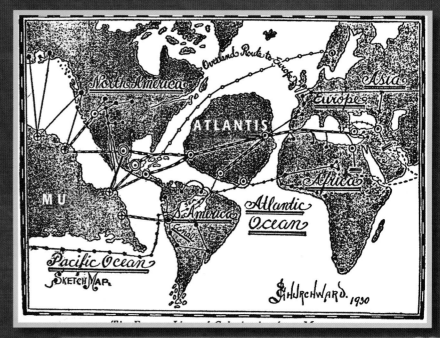

Mythical Quests

Legends of lost civilizations and fabulous riches still entice modern-day explorers. Disbelievers may scoff, but the lands and treasures described on these pages have fired the imagination of adventurers for thousands of years.

North America

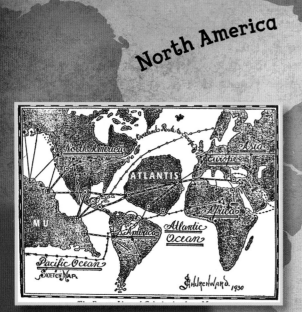

QUEST: **The Lost City of Atlantis**
LOCATION: **Atlantic Ocean, near southern Spain and Gibraltar**

A Greek legend tells of a mighty city, Atlantis, that vanished beneath the sea. In 2011, north of Cadiz, Spain, an American-led research team, using satellite technology, spotted an underwater city, possibly buried long ago by a powerful tsunami. Could it be the fabled Atlantis?

South America

QUEST: **El Dorado, the Lost City of Gold**
LOCATION: **Bogotá, Colombia? The Amazon? The mountains of Ecuador? The border between Brazil and Bolivia?**

In 1541, Spanish Conquistadors set out from Ecuador in search of El Dorado, a jungle city also known as the Lost City of Gold. They failed to find it—and so have the many treasure hunters who came after them. Does El Dorado exist? Now researchers, using Google Earth technology, claim to have seen traces of a huge city in the upper Amazon basin! Stay tuned.

This gold earring was made by an Indian culture that flourished in Colombia between 300 and 1550 A.D. Treasure hunters hope to find more objects like these as they search for El Dorado.

A modern vision of King Solomon's Temple in Jerusalem

Europe

Asia

Africa

QUEST: King Solomon's Treasure
LOCATION: Timna Valley, near Eilat, Israel

King Solomon, ruler of ancient Israel, is said to have been one of the wisest of men—and also one of the richest. Archaeologists are still hunting for the sites of his palaces, perhaps hoping to find some leftover treasure as well.

QUEST: The Lost Continent of Mu
LOCATION: Pacific Ocean, near Hawaii, Fiji, and Easter Island

A 19th-century archaeologist exploring the Mayan ruins of the Yucatán, in Mexico reported finding ancient tablets describing the land of Mu. Mu was an advanced civilization that disappeared somewhere in the Pacific Ocean. Perhaps modern-day archaeologists, using satellite technology, can settle the question once and for all. Did Mu really exist?

Australia

BTW

The movie character Indiana Jones, played by Harrison Ford (above right), was based on Colonel Percy Fawcett. Fawcett disappeared on an expedition to find El Dorado in 1925.

Going for Gold

In the 19th and early 20th centuries, discoveries of gold ore in the western United States led to waves of gold rushes. Tens of thousands of prospectors stampeded to the goldfields to make their fortune. Back then, only a few lucky miners were successful. Today, a new generation of prospectors is heading back to the hills hoping to strike it rich.

Bodacious Mine

LOCATION: Bodie, Washington

Opened in 1897, the Bodie Mine was once a huge operation that produced tons and tons of gold ore for almost a century. Today, teams of new prospectors comb the jagged hills in the area, searching public lands for veins of ore just waiting to be dug up.

Pegleg's Find

LOCATION: The deserts of California or the Santa Rosa Mountains

Panning for gold yields mostly gold dust, which isn't worth much. But it can tell you if there's more gold nearby.

Thomas "Pegleg" Smith was a fur trapper, horse thief, and gold hunter who wandered the West during the mid-19th century. He couldn't stop talking about a place somewhere in a California desert where gold nuggets covered the ground like pebbles. Ever since Smith's death in 1866, true believers have been searching several possible California locations—so far, without hitting pay dirt.

A California mining camp, 1849

BTW

Almost 80 percent of the gold still mined in the United States comes from Nevada. Today, the mining is done by big companies, not by individuals.

The Dutchman's Secret

LOCATION: Superstition Mountain, near Phoenix, Arizona

Many a fortune hunter still believes the old story of a 19th-century German immigrant nicknamed "The Dutchman." He is said to have found a long-lost gold mine in Arizona's Superstition Mountains—but died without revealing its exact location. Could there still be golden treasure in the Lost Dutchman mine?

Blast from the Past

The term *pay dirt* comes from the gold-rush days. It means soil or gravel that contains valuable ore. To "hit pay dirt" was a prospector's way of saying to "strike it rich."

Under the Waves

The *Titanic* may be the best known ship to go down at sea. But there are some smaller, less famous vessels that lie on the ocean floor. And many of them contain valuable treasure.

Silver Sea

LOCATION: 300 miles off the coast of Ireland

Deep in international waters, off the coast of Ireland, a sunken World War II vessel could be holding a huge amount of silver—200 tons, according to old cargo records. The ship has been found by a Florida-based company that is planning to recover the treasure. That much silver could bring the fortune hunters more than $200 million—if those old cargo records are correct!

BTW

For a fee, the website of the International Registry of Sunken Ships will send a report on the whereabouts of one of some 100,000 sunken ships, from submarines to tug boats. But treasure hunters beware: There's no guarantee there are valuables on board.

Catch of Loot

LOCATION: Near the Strait of Gibraltar, between Spain and Morocco

Another rich cargo, $500 million in gold and silver coins, was recently recovered by a private company, from a shipwreck somewhere west of the Strait of Gibraltar. But Spain is claiming the loot, saying the wreck is a Spanish vessel destroyed by a British warship in 1804. It's a good thing that this argument is being fought in court and not on the high seas!

Is Kidd Kidding?

LOCATION: Gardiners Island, Block Island, the Thimble Islands

Treasure doesn't always go down with the ship. Captain William Kidd, an infamous pirate, may have stashed his ill-gotten gains in New York, Connecticut, and Rhode Island in the late 1600s. Many people believe Kidd's loot is somewhere beneath the sands around Long Island Sound, just waiting to be unearthed.

For the Record

UNESCO, a United Nations agency, estimates that there are about 3 million sunken ships on the ocean floor. But probably only about 1,000 of those ships have cargo that is valuable enough to make an expensive recovery operation worthwhile.

Antarctic Adventures

Almost since the world began, daring adventurers have left the comforts of home to explore remote corners of the globe. One of the most challenging destinations was Antarctica, a continent of frozen landscapes that were strangely beautiful—and extremely dangerous. That didn't stop some fearless men in the 19th century from trying to explore it. One of the most famous was Ernest Shackleton.

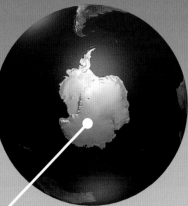

Ernest Shackleton, born in 1874, first goes to sea at age 14 and becomes an experienced sailor. Inspired by the stories of daring British explorers, Shackleton longs to be the first person to reach the South Pole.

Shackleton organizes an expedition to Antarctica. The party comes within less than 100 miles of its goal, but must turn back due to bad weather and low food supplies. "Another 50 pounds of food," Shackleton said, "and we could have made it to the Pole."

1874

1907-1909

1911

To prepare for his own trek to Antarctica, Norwegian explorer Roald Amundsen studies reports of Shackleton's failed expedition. On December 14, Amundsen is the first explorer to reach the South Pole.

Amundsen's account of his Antarctic expedition, published in 1912.

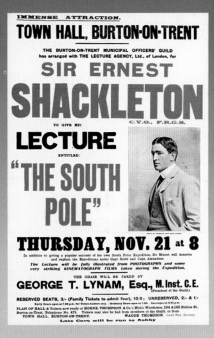

This poster advertises a public talk in which Shackleton announced plans for his second expedition to Antarctica.

An artist's drawing of Shackleton and his men deserting the icebound *Endurance*

From South Georgia
5 DECEMBER 1914

Enters ice pack
(58°-40'-S- 18'-W.)

1000 miles forced through icebergs

Shackleton organizes another expedition, this time, to lead the first group across Antarctica from sea to sea by way of the South Pole. On August 1, Shackleton and his crew set sail from England on a wooden ship, the *Endurance*.

In April, Shackleton and five men set out for a whaling station on another island, 800 miles away, leaving the others behind. Although frostbitten and in rags, they survive the difficult journey across the ocean and over frozen mountain passes. Four months later, Shackleton returns to Elephant Island with a rescue party.

BTW
Shackleton made a total of five expeditions to the Antarctic. Some of the diaries he kept of his adventures are still in print!

1914 1915 1916 1917

From February to October, *Endurance* is trapped in ice near the Antarctic Peninsula. Months later, Shackleton and his crew abandon ship, taking only three small lifeboats, supplies, and sled dogs. Over the next 497 days, they travel across ice floes and rough seas until they reach rocky, uninhabited Elephant Island. Nearly starving, they are forced to eat their dogs.

Every member of the expedition reaches England safely.

Blast from the Past

To recruit 27 men for his crew, Shackleton placed this want ad in the newspapers: Men wanted for hazardous journey. Small wages. Bitter cold. Long months of complete darkness. Constant danger. Safe return doubtful. Honour and recognition in case of success. —Ernest Shackleton

BRITISH ANTARCTIC EXPEDITION 1910
BURROUGHS WELLCOME & Co
LONDON

A medicine kit used by Shackleton during his first expedition and is now at the Science Museum in London.

Sports and Contests

Who's getting serious about snowball fights? How do you race in a bathtub? How many mushy tomatoes can you throw? Come on, fans and athletes! Get your front-row seats to the wide world of weird sports and games!

In This Chapter
- New Twists on Old Games
- Wacky Winter Sports
- Playing with Food

  And Much More!

Strange

Playing chess blindfolded...

Stranger

Flipping pancakes in a footrace…

Strangest

Competing in a Klingon beauty pageant!

New Twists on Old Games

Inventive athletes and contestants are taking sports and games to new levels by changing the rules and creating different versions of old favorites. Some of their creations are really challenging; others are just plain crazy.

Grand Masters Luke McShane (right) and Nigel Short make their moves in blindfolds during a competition in London.

Check Mates!

It's tough enough to play chess without adding obstacles to the game. In blindfold chess, the players have to keep track of each move—in their minds. In simultaneous chess, one player walks from board to board, playing multiple games against different opponents. And when the two types of chess are combined, only a genius can move steadily toward checkmate and win the match.

Ironhearted

Athletes who like their shirts to be neatly pressed can now take part in a crazy new sport: extreme ironing. The challenge is to iron an article of clothing on an ironing board while taking part in an outdoor activity—skiing, spelunking (exploring caves), mountain climbing, or riding a bicycle. Starch or no starch? That's up to the athlete.

Follow the Bouncing Ballplayer

What do you get when you combine volleyball, soccer, gymnastics, and capoeira (cap-o-*way*-rah), the Brazilian martial art that looks like a dance? You get bossaball, which is kind of like volleyball played on a trampoline. Players can bounce up high and really spike the ball over the net. The most famous teams, from Spain and Brazil, have been bouncing around the world, playing exhibition games to introduce the sport to others.

The beaches of Rio de Janeiro, Brazil, are the site of this high-kicking bossaball match.

BTW
Bossaball is a nod to bossa nova, a style of popular Brazilian music.

Wacky Winter Sports

These sports haven't made it to the Winter Olympics. Will they ever?

Dashing Through the Snow

Horse racing is always a thrilling sport. Especially if it's done in the snow with two jockeys, one riding the horse and the other being towed behind the horse—on skis! That type of horse racing, called **skijoring,** began in snowy Scandinavia as a form of winter transportation. Today, skijoring (Scandinavian for "ski driving") is a popular wintertime competition in Montana, where teams made up of a horse, rider, and skier race and slalom down a 700-foot course at speeds that sometimes top 25 m.p.h.

Chill Out!

For some hardy swimmers, a refreshing dip means plunging into icy water. In New York City, members of the **Coney Island Polar Bear Club** gather every New Year's Day to take the plunge into the freezing Atlantic Ocean. Anybody can jump in with them (but if you're under 18, you'll need to bring along an adult willing to freeze with you).

C-1
GREETINGS FROM
CONEY ISLAND
N.Y.
© CURT TEICH B CO., INC.
3B-H1421

Biking the Slopes

If you like mountain biking and skiing, why not go snow biking? Snow bikes have a seat and handlebars, just like a regular bicycle, but they're usually equipped with wider tires that keep the rider's weight evenly distributed. Some bikers think that keeping the tires a little flat gives them better traction in the snow. This is a fun sport, but not a fast one: The average speed for snow biking is about 8 m.p.h.

For the Record

For a faster ride, try ski-biking—bikes that have skis instead of wheels and pedals. The first one, the "Ice Velocipede," was patented in 1892 by inventor J.C. Stevens.

Playing with Food

From the hot-dog-eating contest in Coney Island, New York, to the watermelon-seed-spitting contest in Luling, Texas, food festivals and eating competitions attract some adventurous or very hungry people. Hasn't anyone ever told them not to play with their food?

Flipping Out

It's a tradition that dates back to 1950: the **Pancake Day Race** between the sister cities of Liberal, Kansas, and Olney, England. Held on Shrove Tuesday, the day before Lent, the competition requires racers to carry a pancake in a frying pan as they run a 415-yard course. When they reach the finish line, they flip the pancake to prove they haven't dropped it. So far, Liberal is ahead by several wins, but Olney could flip that around in the years ahead.

A Really Hot Contest

Unless your mouth is lined with a heat-resistant material, this eating competition will truly fire you up. Contestants at *La Costeña* **Feel the Heat Jalapeño Eating Championship Challenge,** held every May in San Antonio, Texas, have 10 minutes to set a record for chomping down jalapeños—a very hot chili pepper. The winner at the 2011 festival managed to swallow 275 whole pickled peppers and walk off with a smokin' $3,000 prize.

Tomato Squish

Every year, on the last Wednesday of August, the Spanish town of Buñol hosts one of the world's wildest food fights: *La Tomatina*. It's a free-for-all where the weapons of choice are tomatoes—more than 90,000 pounds of them. Official tomato-throwers ride through the streets in huge trucks, pelting the crowds along the way with the overripe fruit and getting pelted by the crowds in return. After the slippery, squishy fight is over, everyone washes off in a river.

Atlantic Ocean
FRANCE
PORTUGAL
SPAIN
Buñol
Mediterranean Sea

Ahead by a Nose?

There's nothing like a good old-fashioned footrace. And yet many spectators today are looking for different kinds of racing excitement. So the events are getting stranger and stranger—some of the racers don't even have feet.

Ready, Set, Slow!

A popular sport at village fairs in the United Kingdom, snail racing involves putting a few land snails on a circular track atop a table—and then waiting (and waiting and waiting) to see which one reaches the edge of the circle first. The 2011 champion snail, Zoomer, crossed the finish line in 3 minutes, 23 seconds.

Rub-a-Dub-Tub Race

This odd annual race is part of a festival in Nanaimo, British Columbia, Canada. Contestants (ages 14 and up) ride bathtubs fitted with outboard motors. They must cross the Nanaimo harbor, circle two nearby islands, and then hightail it (or hightub it?) back to the starting point.

Bathtub

The ducky contenders are dumped into the river at the start of a Wisconsin derby.

Just Ducky

You stand to win a prize if your entry comes in first in one of the many duck derbies around the country. All you have to do: Enter your favorite rubber duck, stick a computer-generated number on it, launch it into a river at the starting line (with thousands of competitors), and cross your fingers. The ducks float downstream and the lucky owner of the first lucky duck to cross the finish line wins.

A volunteer member of the clean-up crew pops up among the also-rans.

You Call These Contests?

Competitions aren't just about being smart or clever or having great athletic ability. Some of them involve more unusual talents or achievements. Others don't involve any talent at all.

And the Winner Is...

You may have heard of the Miss America contest, or the Miss Universe contest, but what about the **Miss Klingon Empire Beauty Pageant?** Held in Atlanta, Georgia, as part of the annual TrekTrax convention, this pageant's parade features women who impersonate Klingon characters from the *Star Trek* series or create a Klingon character of their own.

Hop To It

Invented in Sweden in the 1980s, a hare-y new sport has since gone international. **Rabbit hopping** involves training a rabbit to leap over hurdles large and small. Experts say that any breed can learn to jump, but the best contestants are not too big or heavy. Here's one coach's tip: Talking sweetly to your bunny during the event helps keep it calm. In other words, don't make your bunny hopping mad or he or she might not hop at all.

Hairy Situation

This stylish "sport" requires years of prep time—but no practice. At the **World Beard & Moustache Championships**, contestants enter their facial hair in one of several categories, including best natural moustache, and best combination of beard and moustache.

CHAPTER 4

STRANGE BUT TRUE
Inventions

Behind every invention is a dreamer who believed in the impossible. Which of today's strange dreams will become tomorrow's popular inventions? A flying car? A talking mirror that could tell you who is the fairest of them all? Or maybe you have an invention you've been thinking about. It all begins with just one idea!

Strange

A *really* long-lasting light bulb...

In This Chapter

● Stuff that Talks and Texts

● Oddball Innovations

● Inventions Old and New

And Much More!

Stranger

A hummingbird-spy…

Strangest

A gadget for making dimples!

Talking and Texting

The next time you text a friend, think about this: You are using the latest version of a communication technology that once seemed strange to almost everybody—except the inventor. Throughout history, inventors have sought better ways for people to share their thoughts face-to-face or from far, far away. Here's a look at some great communication milestones.

Hold the Wire

Send messages over a wire? American inventor Samuel Morse (1791–1872), believed in that idea long ago. In the 1800s, Morse helped to perfect the single-wire telegraph system, an early method of sending messages over long distances. He was cocreator of the Morse code, a telegraph language that uses dots and dashes.

International Morse Code

1. A dash is equal to three dots.
2. The space between parts of the same letter is equal to one dot.
3. The space between two letters is equal to three dots.
4. The space between two words is equal to seven dots.

Signing In

For centuries, many deaf people couldn't communicate with anyone except through writing or simple motions, such as pointing. Then, in the 1700s, French priest Charles-Michel de l'Epée (leh-*pay*), developed sign language, a system of hand motions that allowed deaf people to communicate with one another and with people who could hear.

Tune In to Marconi

Send messages without a wire? In 1895, a young Italian inventor, Guglielmo Marconi, sent a type of electromagnetic energy over a distance of 1.5 miles. Today, that energy is known as radio waves. About six years later, he transmitted the first wireless signals over 2,000 miles across the Atlantic Ocean. Marconi's wireless telegraph system became a huge success, paving the way for the radios and TVs we enjoy today.

A replica of Marconi's transmitter

AMAZING ADVANCES IN COMMUNICATION

Important dates that helped move civilization forward

3500–2900 B.C. First ALPHABET developed by Phoenicians, a seafaring people living along the Mediterranean

776 B.C. First record of HOMING PIGEONS being used to carry information from one place to another
FACT: The birds were delivering news of the winner of the Olympics in ancient Greece!

105 B.C. PAPER invented in China

1049 A.D. MOVABLE TYPE invented in China by Bi Sheng

1439 PRINTING PRESS created by Johannes Gutenberg
FACT: A printing press could print hundreds of books in a short time. Previously, books were written by hand, or printed from carved woodblocks.

1714 Patent for TYPEWRITER issued to English inventor Henry Mill

1876 ELECTRIC TELEPHONE patented by Alexander Graham Bell
FACT: Bell's first words over the phone were to his assistant: "Mr. Watson, come here, I want to see you."

1877 PHONOGRAPH patented by Thomas Edison

1895 MOVING PICTURE CAMERA and **PROJECTION SYSTEM** created by Auguste and Louis Lumière (Loom-*yare*) in France

1923 TELEVISION CAMERA (cathode-ray tube) invented by Russian-American Vladimir Zworykin

1971 The computer FLOPPY DISK and the **MICROPROCESSOR** (considered a computer on a chip) invented

1973 First MOBILE PHONE call made in the U.S.
FACT: The caller, one of the inventors of the mobile phone, dialed an engineer at a rival company to brag about the new device.

1994 Birth of the WORLD WIDE WEB

2001 Apple Inc. announces creation of the **iPod** portable digital-music player

2007 Apple releases the first iPhone, a cell phone with computing ability
FACT: The iPhone, like other smartphones, added touch screens to cell phones.

2010 Apple releases the iPad, selected by TIME magazine as one of the best inventions of the year

2011–2012 Experiments in MIND READING conducted
FACT: Scientists in California reported that they can identify certain words a person is thinking by "reading" brain waves.

2013 and beyond... What will come next?

Way Cool Inventions

Inventions for improving communication just keep coming. Here is a trio of the latest, chosen by the editors of TIME magazine for their special inventions issue.

Drum Portal

UNICEF'S Digital Drum is designed to help rural communities in Uganda, a country in East Africa, that don't have access to computers. The computer center is preloaded with information about health, education, and other issues. These solar-powered computer kiosks, or stands, are made of metal oil drums that are loaded with educational content. The first Digital Drum was installed at a youth center in the northern Ugandan city of Gulu, and UNICEF plans to deliver the devices to all parts of the nation.

Mirror, Mirror on the Wall . . .

A cool new mirror can show you more than your reflection. Researchers at the New York Times Company Research & Development Lab have built the **Magic Mirror,** which uses a motion sensor to recognize and interact with you. Step up to the glass and it reflects your image; next to your face, you'll see your health history and your daily schedule. You can also ask the mirror to flash the morning news, forecast the weather, and show a to-do list for the day—starting with "Brush your teeth!"

A Touchy-Feely Invention

A company in Finland has come up with an amazing touch screen that enables users to not only touch pictures on the screen, but actually feel them. The company's new **E-Sense** technology uses tixels (a new type of tactile, or touch-sensitive, pixel) to simulate textures from dry and wet to rough and smooth.

For the Record

Studies show that most inventions these days do not come from the fertile brains of lone geniuses. Instead, they result from patient teamwork done at universities and corporations.

Crazy or Cool?

Sometimes inventors get carried away and dream up something so weird it will probably never make it past the prototype, or working model, stage. But who knows? Maybe a few decades from now, one of these designs will be a true success!

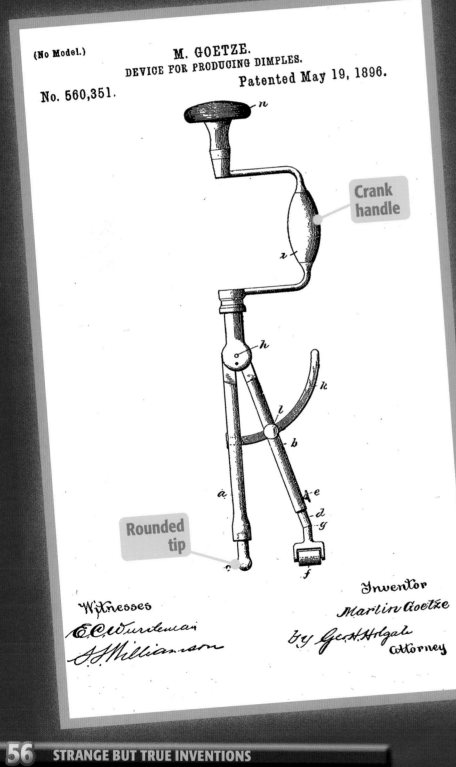

(No Model.)

M. GOETZE.
DEVICE FOR PRODUCING DIMPLES.

No. 560,351.

Patented May 19, 1896.

Crank handle

Rounded tip

Witnesses
E.C. Wurdeman
J.J. Williamson

Inventor
Martin Goetze
by Ge. H. Holgale
Attorney

Turn the Other Cheek

Dimples are cute and make for sweet smiles. But a **dimple-making tool**? Over 100 years ago, that's exactly what one dimple-loving inventor had in mind. In 1896, a design was sent to the U.S. Patent and Trademark Office. It shows a tool with a rounded tip that is meant to be placed against a person's cheek. When a crank handle is turned, it's supposed to create a dimple-like dent on the skin. Ouch!

Giddyup, Dad

Too big for a stroller, but too tired to walk? Ask your dad to give you a ride. The inventor of this **child carrier** thought that older kids might need a lift sometimes. The saddle has stirrups for your feet, but watch out if Dad starts neighing.

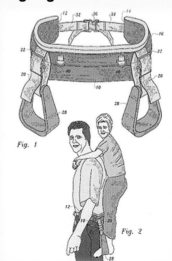

Fig. 1

Fig. 2

By Land, By Sea, By Air

The **Python**, a new type of amphibious automobile, drives like a car on land, and can cruise up to 60 m.p.h. in the water. The Python isn't a new idea. In 1935, H.J. Stone was given a patent for a car-boat-dirigible that could be driven on land, sailed on water, or flown. The vehicle was never produced.

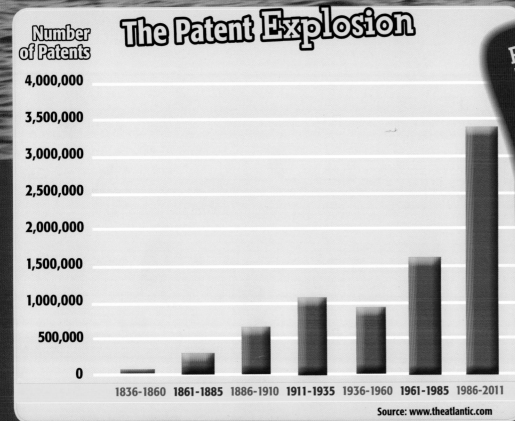

The Patent Explosion

Number of Patents

4,000,000	
3,500,000	
3,000,000	
2,500,000	
2,000,000	
1,500,000	
1,000,000	
500,000	
0	

1836-1860 1861-1885 1886-1910 1911-1935 1936-1960 1961-1985 1986-2011

Source: www.theatlantic.com

For the Record

Got an idea for a far-out invention? Join the crowd! In 2011, the U.S. Patent and Trademark Office issued patent number 8,000,000! One million patents were issued in the previous five years alone.

Just Imagine

A lot of devices we take for granted were once just an idea in an inventor's head. And seeing how fast technology changes, it's a sure bet that within a few years, we'll be adopting new, improved versions of today's cutting-edge inventions.

Yesterday

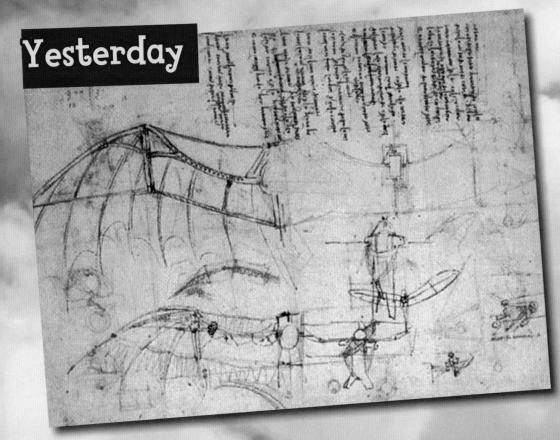

The great Italian artist Leonardo da Vinci (1452–1519), is famous for the *Mona Lisa* and *The Last Supper*. But aviators are interested in his drawings of flying machines—gliders, helicopters, and parachutes. Da Vinci's drawings must have looked really strange to people of his time, but today many of his ideas are a reality.

Today

Over the years, people have used one of da Vinci's sketches as a blueprint to build a to-scale, birdlike flying machine. This model comes close to da Vinci's design—except it's missing the feathers that the artist imagined would cover the frame. Do you think it will fly?

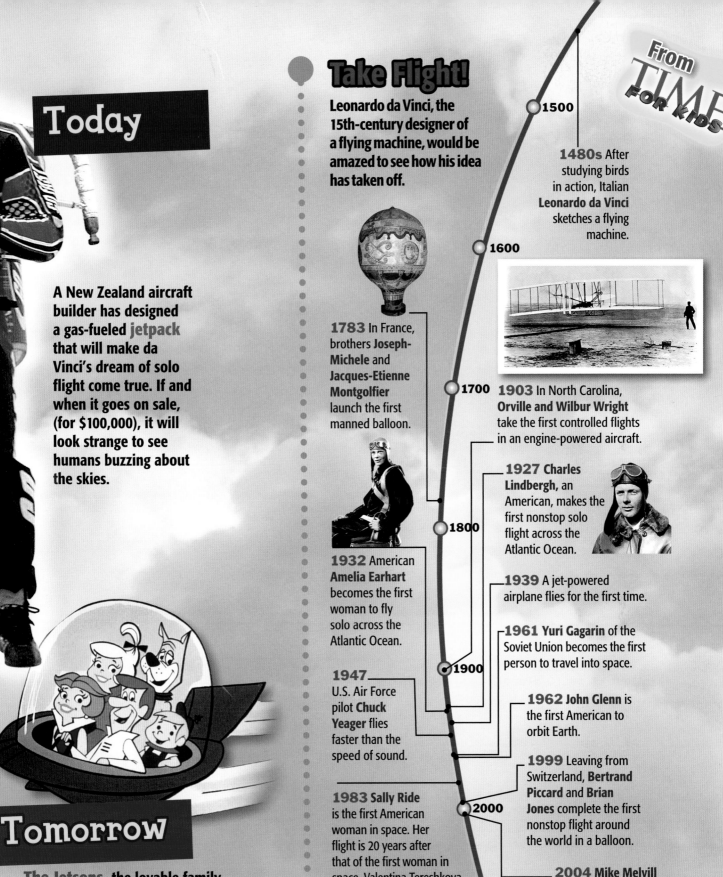

Today

A New Zealand aircraft builder has designed a gas-fueled jetpack that will make da Vinci's dream of solo flight come true. If and when it goes on sale, (for $100,000), it will look strange to see humans buzzing about the skies.

Tomorrow

The Jetsons, the lovable family from the popular TV series, lived 100 years in the future in a wacky world filled with dinosaurs, aliens, and aerocars. Will the Jetsons' flying automobile ever become a reality? Turn to page 64 and find out!

Take Flight!

Leonardo da Vinci, the 15th-century designer of a flying machine, would be amazed to see how his idea has taken off.

1783 In France, brothers **Joseph-Michele** and **Jacques-Etienne Montgolfier** launch the first manned balloon.

1932 American **Amelia Earhart** becomes the first woman to fly solo across the Atlantic Ocean.

1947 U.S. Air Force pilot **Chuck Yeager** flies faster than the speed of sound.

1983 Sally Ride is the first American woman in space. Her flight is 20 years after that of the first woman in space, Valentina Tereshkova of the Soviet Union.

1500

1480s After studying birds in action, Italian **Leonardo da Vinci** sketches a flying machine.

1600

1700

1903 In North Carolina, **Orville and Wilbur Wright** take the first controlled flights in an engine-powered aircraft.

1927 Charles Lindbergh, an American, makes the first nonstop solo flight across the Atlantic Ocean.

1800

1939 A jet-powered airplane flies for the first time.

1961 Yuri Gagarin of the Soviet Union becomes the first person to travel into space.

1900

1962 John Glenn is the first American to orbit Earth.

1999 Leaving from Switzerland, **Bertrand Piccard** and **Brian Jones** complete the first nonstop flight around the world in a balloon.

2000

2004 Mike Melvill pilots *SpaceShipOne,* the first privately launched rocket. The rocket lifts off from California and reaches space.

2100

Going, Going, Gone

People who rode in a horse and buggy must have been astonished to see the first automobile. Imagine how people reacted when a picture projected on a white screen started to move—and then make sounds! New inventions often seem strange until we get used to having them around. And then they are replaced by even more advanced inventions.

The Incandescent Lightbulb

In a world that used torches, candles, and gas lamps for light, it must have seemed like a miracle to flip a switch and see a light go on. That "miracle" was due to Thomas Edison and his incandescent bulb. As electricity flows through the bulb, a wire heats up and starts glowing, producing light.

The incandescent, which people have been using for years, is slowly being replaced by a more energy-saving fluorescent bulb that lasts about 10,000 hours, or 10 times longer than the incandescent.

Now there are LED-based bulbs that give off a warm yellow glow. The bulbs use very little energy and last about 50,000 hours. If they burned 24/7, they'd last for almost six years!

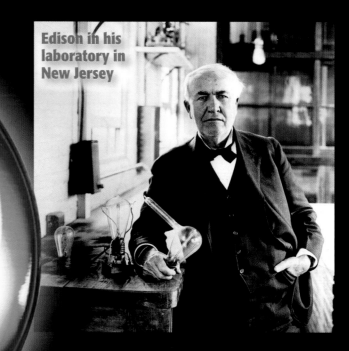

Edison in his laboratory in New Jersey

The Dead Sea Scrolls were written about 2,100 years ago. They contain fragments from most of the books of the Old Testament.

The Book

Before there were books with pages that you could turn, people had to read tablets and **scrolls**. Sometime between the 2nd and 4th centuries A.D., the **codex** (above) was invented. Then, readers could flip back and forth among pages and easily carry their reading material. Will this familiar book form—used for more than 1,700 years—be replaced by **electronic readers**?

To e-read or not to e-read

Dated Inventions

The gas-powered car is on its way out, according to a survey of 500 teens. Take a look at the inventions they say are headed for the trash bags.

Source: Lemelson-MIT Invention Index

1 37% **Gas-powered car**

2 32% **Landline phone**

3 21% **Computer mouse**

4 4% **Other** (includes books, DVDs, VCRs, and radios)

5 3% **Television**

5 3% **"I don't know."**

Take It from Nature

Need a problem solved? Ask Mother Nature. That's the idea behind biomimicry (by-o-*mim*-ik-ree), a term that combines *bio*, meaning "life," and *mimicry*, meaning "to imitate or copy." What biomimicry describes is a way of creating products based on nature's best ideas.

A Bird's-Eye View

It looks and flies like a hummingbird. But don't be fooled. This tiny aircraft, called the Nano Air Vehicle (NAV), is a spying device. The remote-controlled, $4 million NAV has a built-in video camera. Because it is so small, it can go where humans can't. It can scout out safe spots in combat zones, search for earthquake survivors, and even locate a chemical spill. But you won't catch it looking for nectar in a flower.

Biomimicry in Action

Top engineers at German car company Daimler wanted to build a more energy-efficient car. So they headed off to the natural history museum to study sleek dolphins and sharks. But it was the pudgy boxfish that reeled them in: It can start, stop, back up, and zigzag through the water with ease—all with very little energy.

That clumsy-looking fish became their model for creating the new car with an aerodynamic (air-o-die-*nam*-ik) design that reduces wind drag and increases fuel efficiency. The car the team came up with is also modeled on the fish's boxy skeletal system. Thanks to the fish, the car is fast and handles easily, and can run for 70 miles on just one gallon of fuel.

The biologist who coined the term *biomimicry*, Janine Benyus, has worked with cereal companies, speaker designers, and other manufacturers to develop products based on nature's best ideas. "After all," says Benyus, "nature has done billions of years of research to produce well-designed products that last."

A rat's teeth sharpen as they grind against each other. Likewise, these blades sharpen by grinding against metal during use.

Bumpy turbine blades, based on whale fins, capture more wind than smooth ones.

Move Over, Jetsons!

At last, an honest-to-goodness flying car, the Terrafugia (ter-a-*foo*-jee-a) Transition, designed for short trips for work or fun. To take this amazing new vehicle on the road, a driver's license isn't enough. You'll also need to be certified as a sport pilot!

Car of the Future?

Developed by engineers trained at the Massachusetts Institute of Technology (MIT), the Transition production prototype was successfully test-piloted in 2012. So far, almost 100 people have signed up (and paid a $10,000 deposit) to reserve one of the $279,000 car-planes.

BTW

The name Terrafugia is Latin for "escape the Earth"—precisely what the aerocar is designed to do!

On the ground, with wings folded, the gasoline-powered Transition can be driven on any road. Its top speed is about 65 miles an hour.

On its first test flight, the Terrafugia Transition soared to an altitude of 1,400 feet and stayed aloft for eight minutes.

By pressing a button on the control panel, the driver-pilot unfolds the wings.

For the Record

The founder of the Terrafugia company, Carl Dietrich, was inspired to create the car-plane by watching *The Jetsons*. Dietrich had wanted to fly since he was 8 years old, and earned his pilot license when he turned 17.

CHAPTER 5

STRANGE BUT TRUE

Jobs

There are thousands of jobs you can prepare for in school, plus tons of ways to start your own business. But if you crave employment that's a little off-beat, consider one or more of these odd occupations.

In This Chapter

- You Do What??!?!
- Weird Jobs with Animals
- Weird Jobs from the Past

And Much More!

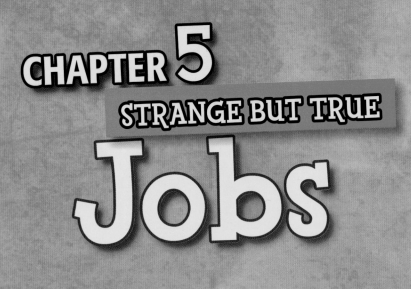

Strange
HELP WANTED:

Fortune-cookie writer...

You will become a successful fortune-cookie writer!

Stranger

HELP WANTED:

Subway people-pusher…

I'D BETTER GET THE PAIL AND BUCKET!

Strangest

HELP WANTED: Poop collector

(in ancient Rome)!

You Do What??!?!

Working nine to five in an office isn't for everybody. Some people prefer jobs that are a little more out-there.

Squeeeeeeeze

JOB DESCRIPTION: Subway Pusher

For people who live in cities with underground transportation, pushing your way onto a crowded train can be hard work. In Tokyo, Japan, riders don't have to do the shoving: That's the job of the oshiya (o-shee-ya), workers who push people through the doors of already-packed subway cars. The oshiya— and the commuters—get a real workout at rush hour, when twice the number of passengers the cars were built to hold try to get onboard.

Hey, somebody's gotta do it!

Whistling Wonders

JOB DESCRIPTION: Professional Whistler

Snow White's favorite dwarves whistle while they work— but for some professionals, whistling *is* their work. It takes perfect pitch, great breath control, and a lot of practice to turn lips and lungs into a musical instrument that can accompany a band or a singer, or carry a solo.

For the Record

Many people are superstitious about whistling. Some Russians believe that whistling indoors will make you lose all your money. Old-time sailors thought that whistling on deck brought bad weather. Many actors fear that whistling backstage will lead to a disaster during their performance.

Fortunate Employment

JOB DESCRIPTION: Fortune-Cookie Writer

Behind every fortune cookie is a fortune writer—a person who has to come up with thousands of maxims, or clever sayings, to print on those little slips of paper. One fortune writer in New York City uses many traditional Chinese sayings, but also finds inspiration in books of proverbs and even subway signs. What's the trick to his trade? "Think in 10-word sentences!" he answers.

Write a Fortune

Here's one way to practice writing maxims for fortune cookies. Choose any 10 words from this chart to construct a mysterious saying. For example, you could write, "Remember to listen for the lucky parrot after the storm." You can also add words of your own.

VERB	PREPOSITION	ARTICLE	ADJECTIVE	NOUN	PRONOUN
beware	after	a, an	orange, blue, red	sister(s)	you
look	of	one	lucky	brother(s)	it
listen	in	the	angry	wizard	we
wait	to	this	happy	parrot	they
remember	for	that	devilish	storm	his/her

Wild Work

Some people would rather work with animals than with people. But they need to pick the right animal if they want to avoid being dinner!

A Job with Jaws

JOB DESCRIPTION: Alligator Wrangler

Wranglers who show off alligators at some of Florida's popular wildlife farms have one of the most dangerous jobs in the U.S. Part of their daily routine is to get the gator to "smile"— that is, open its sharp-toothed mouth so tourists can take photos. Every day the wranglers risk being chomped. One false move, and it's "Later, alligator" for the wranglers.

Feed That Tiger!

JOB DESCRIPTION:
Wild- Animal Handler

If wrangling alligators sounds too hazardous, minding zoo animals may be a slightly tamer option. Still, being a wild-animal handler is hard, dirty work, from keeping cages clean to making sure that the animals are healthy and—for the sake of the workers—not hungry.

Tom, a 14-year-old Bengal tiger in Mississippi, high-fives his handler, signaling he wants to be petted!

Please Don't Bite Me

JOB DESCRIPTION: Snake Milker

It's scary to meet up with a poisonous snake, but snake milkers work with them regularly at a serpentarium, or snake farm. These fearless workers extract, or draw out, the snake's poison by massaging the venom glands, causing the reptile to spit the poison into a jar. The venom is then freeze-dried and shipped to medical facilities. There, it is used to create some medicines, especially antivenin to help save people who were bitten by snakes.

Please Bite Me!

JOB DESCRIPTION: Mosquito Trapper

If you want to help doctors fight malaria, sign up to be a mosquito trapper in Brazil. That's where some fearless researchers expose their skin to lure and then capture the disease-carrying blood suckers so they can be studied in a laboratory. One researcher withstood 3,000 bites in a single, super itchy evening!

BTW

A bite from a malaria-carrying mosquito can be fatal. About 655,000 people, mostly in Africa, died from the disease in 2010.

Bizarre Jobs B.C.

Today's strangest jobs sound pretty ho-hum compared with some of the work people did centuries ago. Ancient Rome, whose mighty civilization has shaped our own, may take the prize for having some of the oddest careers in history.

Going Out with a Smile

JOB DESCRIPTION: Funeral Cheerleaders

Two thousand years ago, when a wealthy person died in Rome, there was a funeral service. And the funeral had a special guest: A funeral clown was hired to walk among the mourners, wearing a mask of the dead person's face and cracking jokes. The idea was to entertain the spirits of the dead and to cheer up the people at the ceremony

SHALL WE CRY? SHALL WE LAUGH?

Curses!

JOB DESCRIPTION: Curse Scribe

Ancient Romans who were angry at someone would hire a curse scribe—a writer-for-hire who transcribed the customer's angry words onto a thin lead tablet. The tablet was then nailed to the walls of altars or temples for everybody, including the "cursee," to read.

Most ancient Romans used public toilets. They provided a place for people to gather and gossip.

No Waste Needed

JOB DESCRIPTION: Poop Collector

Remains of early sewage and plumbing systems are still being used in the modern city of Rome. But if you lived there in the days of the Roman Empire and wanted indoor plumbing, you had to be rich. Poor people usually relieved themselves outdoors, and then counted on the waste-removal services of a *stercorarius* (stir-co-*ra*-ree-us)—that's Latin for poop collector. The stercorarius would travel door-to-door to scoop the poop. Then he sold the waste to farmers who used it as fertilizer.

EXCUSE ME, I NEED TO GO DO LAUNDRY!

Pee-Brained Idea

JOB DESCRIPTION: Clothes Cleaner

In ancient Roman times, slaves called "fullers" were forced to wash woolen garments and other types of cloth. To do their job, the laundry workers had to stand ankle-deep in tubs of urine (that's right: pee), the best cleansing agent known at the time, because its ammonium salts removed stains and dirt. (We don't recommend trying this at home.)

CHAPTER 6

STRANGE BUT TRUE

Science and Technology

Can mice show humans the way to a longer, healthier life? Can objects be teleported from one place to another? Scientists are experimenting with these and other mind-blowing ideas in the laboratory today. Who knows which ones will come true tomorrow?

In This Chapter

- Living Forever and a Day
- Blueberry Brain Power
- Mind-Boggling Bots
  And Much More!

Strange

Bots that play soccer…

Stranger

Cat's ears for people…

???

Strangest

A real-life "invisibility cloak"!

Forever and a Day

Peter Pan never wanted to grow up. Vampires never die. It's strange to say, but there are people today who hope to stay young forever—or if that doesn't pan out, to come back to life after they've died. With the help of scientists, could their plans come true?

How old am I? 78 and counting . . .

A Mouse's Life

Forget living forever. Some people are happy to settle for a long, healthy life. Scientists at Harvard Medical School, in Massachusetts, are taking the first steps to help humans live longer. In an experiment, researchers turned old, creaky mice into healthy animals by injecting them with an enzyme—a type of protein that triggers a chemical reaction—that repaired their bodies. Now, the scientists have to figure out if mice treated with the enzyme will truly live longer, healthier lives. If they do, it might mean that humans would react in a similar way. But that's a long way off.

Gone Today, Here Tomorrow?

Scientists haven't figured out how to bring people back to life. But some hopeful men and women are counting on the technology of tomorrow to do just that. They are believers in cryogenics, a method for suspending newly dead bodies in supercold liquid nitrogen to preserve them until they can be revived by future medical discoveries. The Cryonics Institute, a group dedicated to freezing bodies, houses more than 100 humans and about 90 pets in a cryogenic state.

Blueberry Brain Power

Could a berry be the answer to a healthy life and an active brain? After years of studying blueberry-eating rats in the laboratory and blueberry-eating people in the world, some scientists are convinced that blueberries are "brain berries" that protect our brain cells from damage and memory loss. The secret ingredient, these researchers say, are flavonoids, chemical compounds also found in soy milk, tofu, and— listen up, chocolate lovers!—cocoa. But forget blueberry pancakes or blueberry pie: Cooking the berries may destroy their helpful flavonoids.

For the Record

The longest human life span ever recorded was that of a French woman, Jeanne Calment, who was born in 1875 and died in 1997—a life of 122 years and 164 days.

Bots
On the Move

Robots change, grow, and become more advanced as bot technology advances. The newest models are capable of doing tasks that seemed impossible only a few models back.

Bots at Home

A toy company has created several models of the Robosapien, a clever toy robot that does a lot of things that *Homo sapiens,* or humans, does: lie down, sit up, wave, dance, karate-chop—even burp and whistle! The bot also features a sound-detection system that enables it to talk back when given a command.

Bots in the Air

Live wires are obviously too dangerous for humans to walk on. Workers who are hired to inspect power lines have to shut down the electricity first. That's why a company in Tokyo, Japan, is developing the Expliner, a robot that can "walk" along a live power line without getting fried.

Bots in Bed

Snoring is not only annoying, but it can cause serious breathing problems. Now, snorers can hope for a good night's sleep—when they cuddle up with a **pillowbot**, a Japanese-made robot that looks like a polar bear. When the bot hears loud snoring, it is programmed to rub its paw against the snorer's cheek. This causes the person to change position and breathe normally—until the next snore, and the next paw swipe.

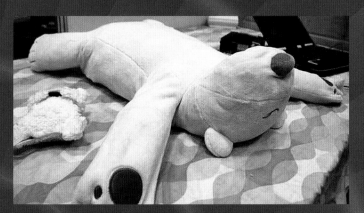

For the Record

One of the world's first humanlike robots, Elektro, built by the Westinghouse Electric Company, appeared at the 1939 New York World's Fair. Elektro was seven feet tall, weighed 265 pounds, walked, talked—and conducted music.

Bots in Sports

The next big soccer star may not be human! At RoboCup 2011, an international robotics competition, the remote-controlled soccer-bot **CHARLI-2** defeated Singapore's Robo Erectus. Despite being slow as a turtle, **CHARLI-2**, created at Virginia Tech by Dennis Hong, earned the Best Humanoid award for its robo-legwork! Engineers hope the bots will be able to defeat human players by 2050.

Thinking Outside the Box

Scientists and engineers are constantly trying to solve the many problems that arise in our high-tech world. Some of their inventions imitate complex natural phenomena; others evolve from simple, and somewhat strange, ideas.

Sunny Solution

Enough solar energy strikes the Earth's surface every hour to power the world for a year. Nature has a unique system for storing that energy for later use: photosynthesis. Taking a hint from nature, Daniel Nocera, a professor at the Massachusetts Institute of Technology, has created an **artificial leaf**. It turns solar energy into storable fuel that can be tapped later as an energy source. Some scientists say that Nocera's leaf is even better at photosynthesis than the real deal!

The artificial leaf is actually a thin silicon solar cell that does the same job as a natural leaf. It doesn't need wires or a battery—just water and sunlight!

For the Record

What are the ingredients in photosynthesis? Using the energy from the sun, plants combine water from the soil and carbon dioxide in the air to synthesize glucose, a carbohydrate that the plants store and use for fuel. Best of all, we get back some of that energy when we eat the plants!

Cloudy Solution

The 2022 FIFA World Cup is scheduled to be played in Qatar—where temperatures in the summer can go above 100°F. What to do? Local engineers propose floating **huge fake clouds** over the stadium during the soccer matches. The shady clouds—lightweight carbon structures filled with helium—could be moved into just the right position by remote-controlled, solar-powered engines. (Of course, if that idea doesn't work, the World Cup could always be rescheduled for wintertime!)

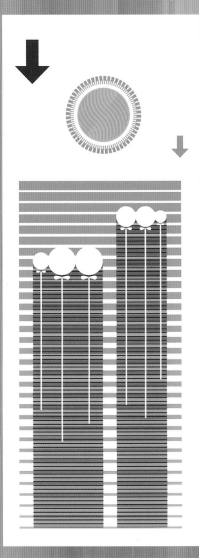

Quick and Easy Solution

Energy-conscious folks who want solar panels to power their building need a good place to put them. The problem: The panels are rigid and have to be installed in carefully angled layers. The solution: A Colorado company, Ascent Solar, invented **thin-film solar panels** (shown above) that can roll and unroll like a carpet. Because the panels can be easily rolled into building materials, a roof or a wall could be made entirely of solar cells, ready to soak up all the power of the sun.

Thin-film solar panels on top of the tent can power lights or charge batteries inside the tent.

Weird Science

Dr. Frankenstein may have been just a character in a novel, but some of his ideas don't sound so strange now. His modern-day counterparts are taking on the challenges of life and death, mental telepathy, and the stuff that dreams are made of.

Mind to Mindflex

Mentalists claim they can read minds, but the true mind readers are neuroscientists, who study how our brains work. Some neuroscientists today are working on technology called brain-computer interface (BCI), which digitizes brain waves and channels their power into video games and computers. One popular game, the **Mindflex**, relies on a BCI headset that allows players to steer a ball through an obstacle course—partly with their thoughts!

Not Seeing Is Believing

Harry Potter's invisibility cloak enabled him to vanish from dangerous situations. But is the cloak just a fantasy? Perhaps not. Scientists at Duke University, in North Carolina, have created a real-life invisibility cloak. This cloak is made of "metamaterials"—artificial materials not found in nature. They deflect the electromagnetic light waves around an object, making it appear to disappear!

Dream On

Here's something to dream about tonight: Scientists at the University of California, Berkeley, want to "watch" the pictures in people's minds. In an experiment, they asked volunteers to look at movie clips while their brain activity was recorded by a special scanning machine. The brain waves were then translated into images with the help of a computer program. The scientists believe that if they can use technology to "read" people's minds, they'll be able to help stroke victims, and others who cannot speak, to communicate through mental pictures.

Left: a scene from a movie. Right: the image produced by scanning the brain waves of a volunteer who is watching that scene.

From Here to There

As every Trekkie knows, when you're about to be "beamed down," you will be instantly teleported to another location. How about in the real world? A team of American physicists recently succeeded in teleporting a photon, a particle of energy that carries light, a little over a yard and creating an identical photon at the end of the journey. What's the point? For one thing, sending data through space will happen a lot faster if physicists can figure out how to "beam" information from one place to another.

BTW

The idea behind teleportation is to take apart the atoms of an object in one location and then send the "blueprint" of that object's atomic makeup to another location, where it will be formed again.

What on Earth Are You Wearing?

One of these days, that question will take on a whole new meaning—thanks to scientists and fabric makers who are messing with chemicals, molecules, and materials. Pretty soon, you won't have to take care of your clothes—they will take care of you!

Safer in the Surf

Surfers who take on big waves take big risks. But with new wet-suit technology, they have a better chance of surviving a wipeout. The lifesaving wet suit has a rip cord. When the cord is pulled, a sac sewn into the back fills up with carbon dioxide, lifting the wearer quickly back to the surface.

Germ-Free Forever?

Many people are more worried about getting germs on their clothes than they are about getting rained on. Now, they can stop worrying. Scientists at the University of Georgia have developed a long-lasting spray that keeps clothes germ-free—no matter how many times they're put through the washer. The spray could be especially useful to keep bacteria off of hospital gowns and athletic gear.

3-D Fashion

Dutch designer Iris van Herpen combines design and technology to make otherworldly dresses. Her first design for an outfit is created through Photoshop. The next step is to work with an architect to develop a 3-D model, which is then printed onto synthetic material. The result is a ready-to-wear dress that is an exact copy of the Photoshop design.

BTW

Photoshop is a software program commonly used by graphic designers and artists to create or edit digital images.

Don't Spill the Milk!

German fashion designer Anke Domaske needs every drop to create QMilch, a silky fabric made from sour milk. First, she extracts strands of protein from the milk; then, she spins the fibers into yarn. All it takes to make a dress or a shirt is a little more than 6 quarts of milk.

Curious and Curiouser

Every year, the editors of TIME FOR KIDS and TIME magazine choose new technologies and gadgets that they think are unique and brilliant, and yes, sometimes strange. Here are just a few of them!

Hands Up!

Technologists in Japan have created an armband that can control a person's hand movements! The device, called **PossessedHand,** is equipped with 28 electrodes that send electricity through joints and muscles, producing precise, involuntary finger movements. Developers say that the armband can help people move a paralyzed limb, and even pluck the strings on a guitar or other musical instrument.

Cat's Got Your Ears

Scientists in Japan have created a **cat-eared headband** that's powered by brain waves. The unusual headband shows the world what you're feeling: The ears perk up when you're excited or concentrating, and drop when you're relaxed. And if you're concentrating and relaxing at the same time, the ears perk up and wiggle.

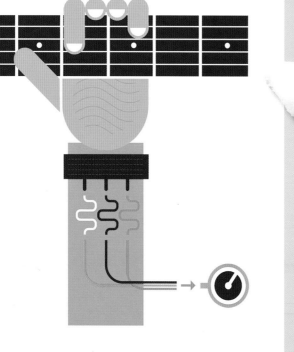

The Next-Gen Pen

What happens if you lose a drawing you made. or if your dog ate it? Help is on the way, with the Inkling pen. It automatically remembers whatever you last drew with it! Using ultrasonic and infrared technologies, the pen captures your sketch line by line, storing it on a receiver that you place on your drawing paper. When you connect the receiver to a computer, it transfers those images as files and—presto!—your lost sketch is now a digital image.

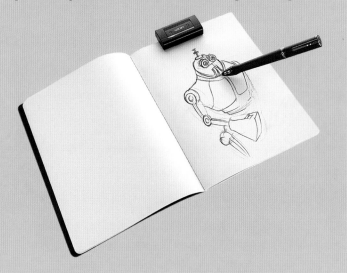

A Map in 3-D

The Urban Photonic Sandtable Display is a full-color holographic map. A holograph is a 3-D image. Software creates the map using information from the real location. Then, lenses re-create the buildings and land features in full color—no 3-D glasses needed! The map displays are up to one foot tall.

Elementary, My Dear Watson

We often take for granted that computers can do astounding things—but win a million dollars on a TV quiz show?! In 2011, an IBM computer named Watson challenged two *Jeopardy* champions, Ken Jennings and Brad Rutter, and it finished first! Although Jennings and Rutter knew a lot of stuff, they didn't stand a chance against a computer that could zip through 200 million pages of facts and figures in seconds. Happily, Watson donated all its winnings to charity (that was IBM's idea, not the computer's).

Art

Strange

An umbrella hat…

What is art? It's a picture of stairways and strange creatures. It's a dress made from a tasty dessert. It's a creation inspired by a weather map. These are only a few of the strange but artful ideas you're about to discover.

In This Chapter

● **Impossible Objects**

● **Science and Art**

● **Oddball Clothes**

And Much More!

Stranger

A monster that prowls beaches…

Strangest

A dot-crazy room

Wonderfully Strange

Some artists like to paint pretty pictures or make beautiful sculptures. Others see the world as a weird and mysterious place—and their artwork turns out to be as strange as their vision.

Throwaway Materials

Growing up in New York City, Tara Donovan must have seen a lot of litter. Maybe that's why she uses so many disposable items—from Styrofoam cups and paper plates to rolls of Scotch tape—to make her artwork. Out of these odd and not very long-lasting materials, Donovan manages to create beautiful things. In *Untitled* (2003), shown here, she uses a familiar object. Can you tell what it is? Hint: You can pour coffee into it. (The answer is at the bottom of the page.)

Answer: Styrofoam cups

Seeing Is Not Believing

Some of the most popular—and puzzling—prints in the 20th century were made by Dutch artist M.C. Escher (1898–1972). His most famous works are optical illusions, such as drawings of impossible structures and buildings, and staircases that go on and on.... *House of Stairs* features weird creatures slinking up and down multiple stairs. How many stairs do you see? (The answer is at the bottom of the page.)

BTW

Escher's work makes use of tessellation, a geometric design that repeats a shape over and over again without any gaps or overlaps.

Answer: 11

Beach Artwork

Beachcombers come across some pretty strange things along the shoreline, but nothing as unusual as the magical moving creatures created by Dutch artist Theo Jansen.

Theo Jansen has been making beach animals for more than 20 years. His creatures look like giant dinosaur skeletons come to life. Powered by the wind, the sculptures appear to be walking.

The beach animals are a form of kinetic, or moving, sculpture. The creatures move by creating their own energy. The plastic tubes fit one inside the other and slide back and forth. This forces air in and out of the tubes, building pressure that creates movement.

Theo Jansen studied physics in college, and he uses his scientific knowledge to create his artwork.

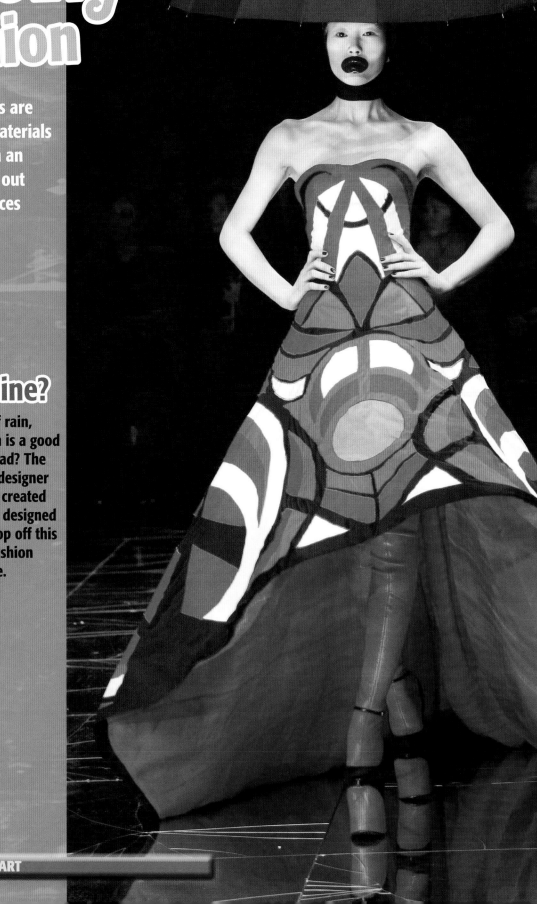

Wacky Fashion

Clothing designers are artists who use materials to dress people in an artful way. Check out these unusual pieces of clothing.

Rain or Shine?

If there's a chance of rain, carrying an umbrella is a good idea—but on your head? The late British clothing designer Alexander McQueen created a sensation when he designed an umbrella hat to top off this colorful gown at a fashion show in Paris, France.

And for Dessert . . .

Here's the question: Is an outfit made from 1,500 cream puffs in good taste? A Ukrainian pastry chef seemed to think so. It took him two months to put the dress together for his bride. Let's hope her supersweet garment didn't attract too many flies.

All Zooted Up

In the 1930s and 1940s, the totally cool zoot suit was popular among hip dudes, especially those who played music or hung out in the jazz clubs of Harlem, a lively African-American neighborhood in New York City. Several clothing makers claimed credit for inventing the long, oversize jacket and high-waisted, wide-legged pants.

BTW

During World War II, U.S. government officials condemned the big, baggy zoot suit. They thought it was a waste of material that was needed for military purposes!

A member of the hip-hop group the Sugarhill Gang wears a zoot suit.

Dot's All, Folks!

In Brisbane, Australia, artist Yayoi Kusama invited children to place thousands of polka-dot stickers anywhere they wanted in an all-white room. The result is a work of art called *The Obliteration Room*.

The room started out like this . . .

. . . and then the children began sticking on polka dots…

. . . and after two weeks: the final product!

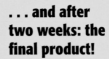

BTW

Why did the artist call this *The Obliteration Room*? To obliterate means to wipe out or blot out. What was blotted out by all those polka dots? Do you see a place to put any more dots?

It's Not a Science, It's an Art

Many artists who are inspired by nature paint landscapes, animals, and bowls of fruit. Others get their ideas from science and the forces of Mother Nature, with some very strange results.

Seeing Science in Color

Rain or shine, Nathalie Miebach collects data on barometric pressure, and other measurements related to meteorology. But Miebach isn't a forecaster: She's an artist who translates weather patterns into awesome art. Her goal, she says, is to help people understand scientific information in a different way. One of her works, *The Perfect Dance,* uses pinwheel shapes to show how two storms collided to form "The Perfect Storm," a horrendous hurricane that struck the northeast coast of the U.S. in 1991.

Back to the Future

The 19th century was a time of great discoveries and imaginings. Inventors from James Watt to Robert Fulton created new types of engines that used the power of steam. Writers such as Jules Verne and H.G. Wells described technologies that didn't yet exist—but would. Scientists and mathematicians like Charles Babbage and Ada Lovelace hatched plans for computerlike machines. Drawing on the visions of these giants, a group of artists today work in what they call the "steampunk" style, combining the past and the future to make sculptures, machines, costumes, and drawings.

Artist Alex Holden created this sculpture with gold paint and bits of junk. He says it's modeled after a 19th-century sewer-cleaning machine, and he named it "Dalek," for its resemblance to the mutants on the British science-fiction TV series Dr. Who.

Making the Impossible Possible

The **Penrose triangle**, or tribar, is a geometric object that is seemingly impossible to make. Look at the diagram and you'll see why: The sides of the triangle could never come together. For years, artists have been challenged to make a three-dimensional tribar. An artist in Perth, Australia, may actually have succeeded.

CHAPTER 8

STRANGE BUT TRUE

Buildings

The places some folks call home can be pretty unusual. Imagine living in a nautilus shell. Or a modern-day castle with wild animals on the lawn. Check out these and other jaw-dropping buildings!

In This Chapter

- Home, Strange Home
- A Mad, Mad, Mad Hotel
- A Building or a Sculpture?

  And Much More!

Strange

A town with an Eiffel tower, a pyramid, and a sphinx…

Stranger

A building shaped like an enormous parasol...

Strangest

A house that's upside-down!

Home Strange Home

The dwellings we call home come in all shapes and sizes, but few look as strange as these.

Home Wrecker

Could a tornado have upended this house? Nope. This is exactly how its owner, a businessman from a small village in Poland, designed it. Some people say he wants to make a statement about the topsy-turvy state of the world today.

Curled Up for the Night

What's it like to live in a giant seashell? This fanciful house in Mexico City might give you an idea. Its design resembles the beautiful curved shell of the chambered nautilus, a mollusk related to the squid and the octopus. Inside this concrete nautilus are stone walkways, a carpet made of grass, and a bathroom with sandy walls.

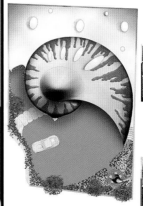

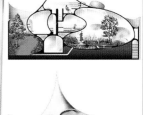

Meet a Nautilus

From TIME FOR KIDS

Below is the shell and the home of a real chambered nautilus.

A. The nautilus's **eyes** do not have lenses. Water can flow in and out of the eyes.

B. The nautilus has up to 47 pairs of **tentacles**, which it uses to smell and to handle food.

C. Inside the nautilus's striped shell, there are **chambers**, or sections, that form a spiral. The animal lives in the chamber closest to the shell opening. As it grows, it adds more chambers.

D. When in danger, the nautilus can pull itself completely into its shell and seal itself in by closing its tough **hood**.

E. The nautilus's **shell** is thick and hard. It has stripes on the outside. Inside, the shell is shiny.

Modern Fantasies

History books tell of majestic buildings: the temples of Egypt, the palaces of Babylon and China, and the tombs and fortresses of India, just to name a few. Some modern builders dream of re-creating the fantastic structures of the past.

Viva Las Vegas!

Las Vegas, Nevada, is a city with many eye-catching structures that were built to look like famous buildings from different parts of the world. Wander down the main street, called the Vegas Strip, and you'll spot a replica of the Eiffel Tower, a giant re-creation of a Roman palace, and, best of all, the **Luxor**—a glass hotel in the shape of an Egyptian pyramid, complete with **concrete Sphinx**.

Hearst named his castle *La Cuesta Encantada*, Spanish for "The Enchanted Hill."

The building alongside the Neptune Pool is an ancient Roman temple that Hearst had shipped to California from Italy.

It's a Mad, Mad, Mad Hotel

The 10-story Tianzi Hotel, in the small town of Langfang, China, clearly takes the prize for weirdness. It's made up of three Chinese gods: Shou (left), the symbol of longevity; Fu (middle), who stands for good luck; and Lu (right), who represents prosperity. Look closely at the peach in Shou's hand and you'll see the windows of the hotel room that's inside it.

Window

An American Castle

"A man's home is his castle" is an old saying that fits William Randolph Hearst to a T. Hearst, who ran a chain of newspapers in the early 1900s, built his outsize version of a Spanish fortress on 250,000 acres of land high above the central California coast. In Hearst's day, zebras, camels, kangaroos, and other wild animals roamed the surrounding hills. Today, Hearst Castle is a state park where visitors can tour some of the 165 richly decorated rooms and stroll through the beautiful grounds.

A Shady Structure

The **Metropol Parasol**, in Seville, Spain, is the world's largest wooden urban construction. The umbrella-like design provides shade from the hot sun. English speakers liken the structure to a parasol, or umbrella. But in Spanish, it's called *Las Setas de la Encarnación* (the mushrooms of Encarnación Square). Which does it look like to you?

SPAIN
• Seville

The Parasol is about 85 feet high and was completed in 2011.

The wafflelike roof is made of timber coated with polyurethane, a type of resin that protects the wood.

The Parasol has four floors. At the top are terraces and a restaurant that overlook the medieval center of Seville. A farmer's market is on the street level. Underground is a small museum that displays Roman ruins and ancient artifacts discovered at the site.

BTW

The Parasol was designed by a team led by the German architect Jürgen Mayer. Mayer must like undulating, or wavy, buildings. Here's another of his creations, part of a food factory in Denmark.

On and Off the Drawing Board

Can you imagine what tomorrow will look like? Some visionary architects have designs for daring new constructions on the drawing board. Other builders have already made their wildest dreams a reality—and are changing the landscapes of the world's cities and towns.

Building Blocks

Several years ago, an international team of architects, led by the world-famous Rem Koolhaas, unveiled designs for the stupendous Interlace House in Singapore, a city-state in southeast Asia. This giant complex will be made up of 31 apartment blocks that are stacked like—well, like blocks—in a nest of greenery. The project, now under construction, will create 1,040 apartments for some lucky homeowners.

Twisted Skyscraper

The tallest skyscraper in Kuwait City, Kuwait, doesn't look like a skyscraper at all: It looks more like a giant, curving sculpture. The 1,354-foot **al-Hamra Tower** faces the Persian Gulf and has its back to the Arabian Desert. To protect it from the glaring heat of the sun, the builders wrapped the tower in glass and then covered the south side with a layer of limestone. The building's 130-degree curve traces the sun's path across the sky.

CHAPTER 9

Body Feats

Can you wiggle your ears? Curl your tongue? Rap out a tune on your head? No big deal. Take a look at the really, really strange things some really, really unusual people do with their bodies!

In This Chapter

- Crazy Contortionists
- Daring Stunt People
- Real Fakirs

  And Much More!

Strange

A slithery snake woman...

Stranger

A Ferris-wheel walker…

Strangest

A man in a box!

Limber Up!

Contortionists are super-gymnasts who can bend their arms, legs, and backs into what look like impossible shapes. How do these human pretzels do it? It takes flexibility and years of tough training.

Human Pretzel

Alexey Goloborodko (Al-ix-*ey* Ga-la-ba-*rroj*-ka) is one of the world's most awesome contortionists. Known as "Bendy Boy," he travels the world in a show that features acrobats and contortionists.

BTW

Some people think that contortionists have twice the number of joints—the places where bones meet and join together. That's a myth. Everybody has the same number of joints. But most contortionists, like gymnasts, are naturally limber. Other people can develop that kind of flexibility, but only after years of intense practice.

Snake Girl

The South African contortionist Lunga calls herself "Snake Girl." Can you see why?

Frontbend

Backbend

Body Benders

There are basically two types of contortionists: the **back-benders** and the **front-benders**. Only a few can bend in both directions.

Blast from the Past

This young American contortionist was photographed doing a backbend in 1880.

Jack-in-the-Box?

Some contortionists can fold up into incredibly small spaces.

Now turn the page and see what body feats you can do!

Can You Do It?

There are some body feats that a few people can do, even if they're not contortionists. Check off the ones you can do.

I can...

☑ Twitch my nose

☑ Wiggle my ear

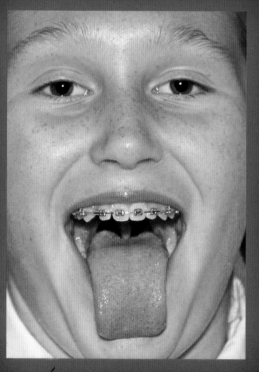

☑ Touch my nose or chin with my tongue

☑ Pull my legs behind my head

☑ Pat my head and rub my stomach at the same time

☐ Pull my inner eyelids over my eyes

✓ Raise one eyebrow at a time

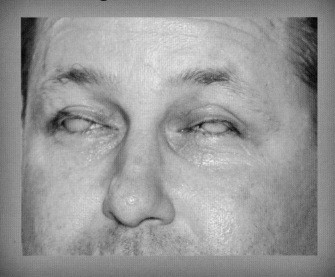

✓ Lick my elbow

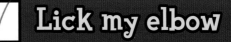

✓ Stand on one foot with my eyes shut and count to 50

How did you do? Check out the score:
0-3: Need More Gym
4-8: Master Pretzel
All 9: Contortionist Extraordinaire!

Super Stunts

Super-heroes use their super-powers to pull off jaw-dropping stunts. But there are plenty of all-too-human performers and circus stars who develop their own incredible powers, through gymnastic training, lots of practice, and a fearless attitude.

Super Heroes in Action

Stunt people often take the place of stars in movies that require dangerous feats. Others thrill crowds at fairs and shows. This stunt performance, at the grand opening of a high-rise hotel in Bangkok, Thailand, features a cast of daredevil Spider-Men sliding down the walls of the building.

Tightrope Without a Rope

A seventh-generation member of the famous acrobatic family known as the "Flying Wallendas," Nik Wallenda doesn't need a wire to do his high-level walking. A Ferris wheel is just as handy!

For the Record

The Wallenda family comes from a long line of jugglers, animal trainers, clowns, and tightrope walkers. Starting out as a small German circus troupe in 1780, the Wallendas became famous in the 20th century for heart-stopping aerial stunts. Several branches of the Wallendas are still thrilling circus audiences today.

Man on a Wire

Breaking his own world record, Swiss tightrope artist **Freddy Nock** walked the 3,264-foot cable-car rope leading to Germany's highest mountain.

Lufthansa

lufthansa.com

Walking on Air

Walking a mile or two every day gives the body a good workout. But strange to say, some men and women prefer to do their walking a mile or two up in the air.

Blast from the Past

On July 8, 1876, Italian tightrope walker Maria Spelterini became the first and only woman to walk a tightrope about 200 feet above the Niagara Gorge, a waterway that separates the United States from Canada. On a second trip across (small photo, right), she walked with peach baskets on her feet!

How Weird Is This?

In parts of Asia and Africa, as well as some Western countries, crowds often gather around people who have trained their bodies to undergo strange—and incredible—trials.

No Time for Sleeping

Lying in bed is a challenge for some people: the men and women who make a practice of stretching out on needle-sharp nails. India has traditionally been the home of these thick-skinned folks who have learned to distribute their weight evenly on nail-studded planks—and who always make sure all the nails are rust-free!

No Hiccuping Allowed

In southwestern China, a kung fu master demonstrates the art of sword-swallowing at a festival celebrating the Chinese New Year. The act is not a trick. The performer slides the blade—whose sharp edges and points have been dulled—right down his throat! Please don't try this at home!

Just How Hot Is It?

David Willey, a physics professor in Pittsburgh, Pennsylvania, collects data about firewalking. Here, he hotfoots it along a 165-foot bed of burning coals while his assistant takes temperature readings with an infrared meter.

BTW

Kids who visit the Discovery Science Center in Santa Ana, California, can get firsthand experience lying on a bed of 3,500 nails!

CHAPTER 10
STRANGE BUT TRUE
Size

Size

Pick your slogan: "Good things come in small packages" or "The bigger, the better!" Or do you prefer the notion of strange things that come in packages big and small? Here are some of the strangest.

Strange

A chess piece that might melt in your hand…

In This Chapter

- A Pencil for a Giant
- A Two-Fish Aquarium
- A Sheep that Weighs 106 Tons

  And Much More!

Stranger

A teeny-tiny car for a teeny-tiny driver…

Strangest

The biggest, gummiest gummy worm ever!

Big Stuff

From whopping burgers to huge bags of popcorn, supersize stuff is everywhere. But is bigger always better? That depends on the stuff!

Monster Cycle

Motorcycle fans who want to rule the road might consider jumping on this outsize bike with the outsize name: The **Gunbus 410 Cubic Inch V-Twin Motorcycle.** It's 11 feet, four inches long, with a seat that's more than three feet off the ground. At 1,433 pounds, it might be a little hard to handle on the road. But it sure looks like you'd get the ride of your life!

Big thinkers tend to think up big ideas. This supersize pencil might come in handy for writing them down. The pencil is 16 inches long and 4½ inches in circumference, and it actually works, eraser and all!

Actual Size

0 Inch 1

Stupendous Sheep

Australia is home to a huge sheep-farming industry. And where there are sheep, there is wool. One of the finest types of wool comes from merino sheep. To honor them, an Australian wool company built the world's biggest merino ram, nicknamed **Rambo**. The concrete statue is more than 48 feet high (about as high as a five-story building), and weighs 106 tons!

BTW

An average merino ram weighs around 200 pounds.

Small Stuff

Petit, pequeño, piccolo, chiisai, dogo, maliit.* No matter what language you say it in, it still means small. Here are some examples of tiny things.

A Tight Fit

Squeeze into the front, and only, seat of the world's tiniest car! It's the **Peel 50**, based on an original model made by a British company in the 1960s. This "little engine that could," housed in a body that is 4¼ feet long and less than 3½ feet wide, gets up to 118 miles per gallon of gas, and can chug along at about 40 miles per hour.

Almost Invisible

A miniaturist is person who makes tiny works of art. A micro-miniaturist like Russian artist Anatoly Konenko makes art pieces that are even tinier. Konenko recently created an **aquarium** that may be the teeniest in the world. It has just enough room for two teaspoons of water, two tiny fish, and some algae, plantlike organisms that live in the sea.

Actual Size

*French, Spanish, Italian, Japanese, Swahili, Tagalog

Flying Small

If you're up for a solo flight, hop on board the world's smallest manned aircraft, the **Colomban** *Cri-Cri* (*Cri-Cri* is French for cricket). The two-engine *Cri-Cri* holds one passenger and is 12 feet, 10 inches long. These ultralight planes can be built from a kit—although you'd probably want an engineer on hand to help you understand the instruction manual!

Dr. Photo

No need to say cheese! A German company has made a **miniature camera** that's smaller than the head of a matchstick. Doctors use the camera to take pictures of the inside of a patient's body during operations or other medical procedures.

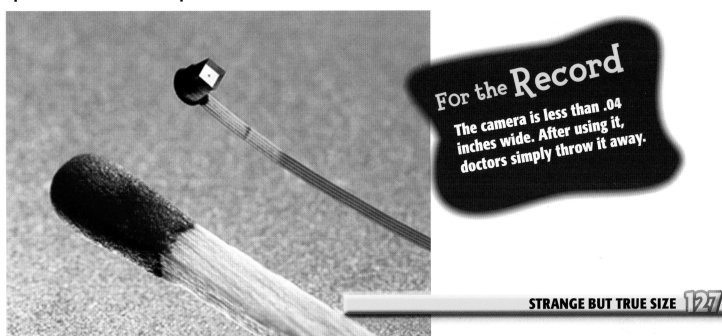

For the Record

The camera is less than .04 inches wide. After using it, doctors simply throw it away.

Outsize and Outlandish

Large or small, some things are almost too strange for words.

Big Cheese

What's the point in wearing a huge hat that looks like a wedge of Swiss cheese? Well, for one thing, it's hole-y. And if someone tells you that you look cheesy, you don't have to feel insulted. Otherwise, there is no point in wearing a 14-inch-wide hat that looks like a wedge of Swiss.

This chess piece, called a rook, was carved to resemble London's famous Big Ben clock tower.

Chess on Ice

Think it's thrilling to play chess? It was actually chilling—when teams of British and Russian chess players faced off in London's Trafalgar Square in January 2007. The chess pieces, carved out of ice, were over three feet high, and placed on a chessboard that was about 690 square feet. Luckily, the pieces didn't melt before the match ended (in a draw).

Sweet Tooth

If you happen to love gummy worms, this one (advertised as the world's largest) is just for you. Each candy is more than two feet long, weighs three pounds, and comes in dual flavors like blue raspberry/red cherry. And it's packed with calories—4,000 to be exact, about the same amount you'd get if you ate 130 regular-sized gummy worms!

CHAPTER 11
STRANGE BUT TRUE
Food

Octopus ice cream, anyone?

Hey, what's for dinner? The answer depends on where you live. A burger and fries? Fish-and-chips? Rice and beans? That's pretty standard fare. Some cultures go in for truly exotic foods. Dig in!

In This Chapter

- Sausage for Vampires
- Pooped-Out Coffee Beans
- Fried Guinea Pig

  And Much More!

Strange

Spaghetti in ink...

MENU

Stranger

A gooey, gluey dish from Brunei…

Strangest

A hard-boiled egg—beak and bones included!

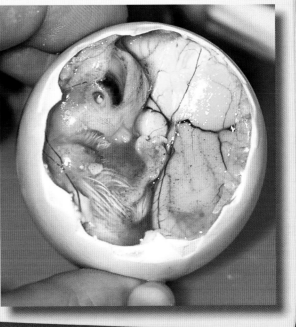

Dish It Out

There are some unusual dishes and drinks popping up on restaurant menus these days. Check out these wacky specials—and place your order, if you dare!

Pasta Dish: Squid Spaghetti

Squid cooked in its own ink is a popular recipe in Italy and Spain, where the black color and strong iodine flavor are truly appreciated. Combining squid and ink in a pasta sauce is relatively new to the United States, but the dish is very popular among pasta lovers.

Main Course: Blood Sausage

It's the perfect entrée for a vampire or a zombie: a mix of dark red blood and pork or another meat, stuffed into a sausage casing. Blood sausage fans say it tastes best when the blood is fresh, not clotted! Want mustard and fried onions on that?

Vegetable: Fiddlehead Ferns

For about three weeks in May, when ostrich ferns in the northeastern United States begin to uncurl, wild-food lovers head for the woods. They snip off the fiddleheads—the tips of the unfolding plants—and sell them to farmer's markets and fancy food stores. Pan-fried in a little butter and salt, the crunchy fiddleheads taste a bit like asparagus tips.

Dessert: **Choice of Bacon or Octopus Ice Cream**

We all scream for ice cream—but what if it's made with candied bacon? Or octopus? That might lead to a different kind of screaming. American chef and cookbook author David Lebovitz whipped up the first sweet-and-salty treat, glazing the bacon with light brown sugar and a pinch of cinnamon. As for the octopus ice cream: It's sold in Japan, where people love the taste of fish, even in their ice cream.

リアスの恵みが
アイスの中に…

たこアイス

種別 アイスミルク250円

乳脂肪分 6.0%

内容量 120ml

MENU

Beverage: **Kopi Luwak Coffee**

Top off the meal with a cup of the most expensive coffee in the world. What makes it so special? The fact that it's brewed from beans that have been eaten, but only partly digested, by coffee-berry-loving animals called civets. The beans are picked out of the civets' poop and then dried, cleaned, and roasted to perfection.

BTW

Civets are catlike mammals found mainly in the Indonesia archipelago—especially on Java, an island whose name is the slang term for coffee!

Strange Tastes

Adventurous eaters sample the local food whenever they visit a new place. They often find dishes that are popular in one country but virtually unknown—or unliked—anywhere else.

I'm ready to cook some yummy balut.

FOOD: Horsemeat
LOCATION: France

Whether served cooked or tartare (raw), horsemeat is often sold by butchers in France. It can also be found on some restaurant menus.

FOOD: Nutria stew
LOCATION: Louisiana, U.S.A.

Fearless eaters in Louisiana are now dining on nutria, a type of swamp rat that is overpopulating the state. Local chefs claim the meat is high in protein and low in fat.

FOOD: Fried guinea pig
LOCATION: Peru, Ecuador, Bolivia

North Americans like to raise them as pets, but in some parts of South America, guinea pigs make tasty dinners!

ny's Specials

FOOD: Drunken shrimp
LOCATION: China

Shrimp swim in a bowl of strong rice wine that cleans the shrimp while adding flavor. And yes, you eat them alive.

FOOD: Ice soup
LOCATION: Korea

Naeng myun (nang myun) is a bowl of shaved ice, vegetables, and noodles, all mixed together. This chilly, soupy dish is especially good for lunch on a hot summer day.

FOOD: Balut
LOCATION: Philippines

Duck eggs that are almost ready to hatch are boiled until they are done. Then they are eaten—bones, beaks, and feathers included.

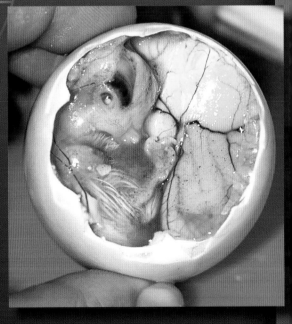

FOOD: *Ambuyat*
LOCATION: Brunei

The traditional meal of Brunei is the fiber from the trunk of the sago palm tree. The fiber is crushed into sawdust and boiled until it looks like rubber cement.

FOOD: Marmite
LOCATION: Australia, England, New Zealand

People in these countries either love or hate this super-smelly breakfast spread made of yeast.

CHAPTER 12

STRANGE BUT TRUE

Ideas

Who was Nikola Tesla—and which of his far-seeing projects challenge inventors today? How do Charles Darwin's theories match up with the science of genetics? Is the universe made of cosmic rings? There are lots of wild ideas out there. Some have come true.

Strange

Mickey Mouse, alchemist!

In This Chapter

- Elementary Magic
- Concentric Universes
- Traveling Through Time

  And Much More!

Strangest

A seven-foot-tall human, aged 120 years!

Stranger

Tesla's wild experiments with electricity…

20th-Century Wizard

Tesla in his laboratory

Nikola Tesla, the brilliant Serbian-American inventor, was one of Thomas Edison's fiercest rivals. Tesla created powerful electrical systems that helped light up the world. But some of his wildest ideas about electricity remain out of reach.

Look, Ma, No Wires!

What would we do without electricity? Unfortunately, we know the answer. If power lines aren't buried underground, storms can bring them down, causing millions of homes and buildings to go dark. Why can't we just get rid of all those electric wires? **Nikola Tesla** (1856–1943) certainly tried. His plan was to send electricity wirelessly across the globe through the electrified upper atmosphere of the Earth. Tesla never proved his idea could work. But he inspired new generations to tackle the problem of wireless electricity—with no luck as yet.

The **Tesla Tower** on New York's Long Island was built from 1901 to 1905. Tesla hoped to use it to send electrical power across the Atlantic Ocean. Due to lack of funding, the tower was never completed.

An inspiration to inventors around the world, Tesla discovered the basis of alternating current (AC) motors, which is how most of our electricity is delivered. He also laid the groundwork for robots, computers, and missile science.

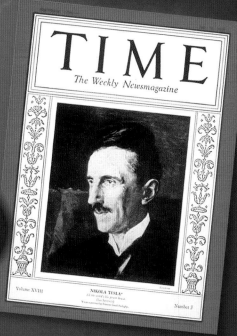

TIME
The Weekly Newsmagazine

Volume XVIII

NIKOLA TESLA

Number 3

Nikola Tesla was featured on the cover of TIME magazine on July 20, 1931.

BTW

In recent years, scientists have tried to use high-powered lasers as energy sources. They also hope to capture solar power and beam it down to Earth. But so far, these ideas, like Tesla's dream of wireless electricity, haven't worked on a large scale.

A Tesla fan in Australia shows off his homemade Tesla coil, a producer of high-voltage AC electricity. Modern versions of the coil, first created by the inventor over a century ago, are still in use.

Fiction to Fact?

Within the next 100 years, will scientists turn the ideas of fiction writers and filmmakers into reality?

Elementary Magic

Harry Potter's creator, J.K. Rowling, once said: "To invent this wizard world, I've learned a ridiculous amount about alchemy." For centuries, alchemy was the stuff of fairy tales, a magical way of turning cheap metals, such as lead and iron, into precious gold and silver. Today's alchemists are nuclear physicists who can actually transmute, or change, one element into another by changing the number of protons in the element. To do that, however, takes so much nuclear energy that the cost is not worth the effort!

Even Mickey Mouse has dabbled in magic, in Walt Disney's *Fantasia.*

Au
Gold

BTW

An element is a substance, such as gold, silver, or lead, with a specific atomic number that indicates how many protons are in each of the element's atoms. Lead has 82 protons and gold has 79. In theory, by adding or subtracting a few protons, one element can be changed into the other!

Pb
Lead

Here is Albus Dumbledore in his lab, a scale model of the movie set.

Master Alchemist

In the Harry Potter series, Albus Dumbledore, headmaster of Hogwarts School of Witchcraft and Wizardry, is said to have learned alchemy by working with a man named Nicolas Flamel. The real Flamel lived in France in the late 14th and early 15th centuries. Many people of the time believed that he unlocked the secrets of alchemy by using a magical Philosopher's Stone. But J.K. Rowling may be the world's most successful alchemist: She turned her imagination into gold!

TOP 5

Books About Time Travel

Time travel is an idea that may yet happen—if you believe the physicists who are studying the possibilities. But until they prove their theories, the best way to travel through time is to read one or more of these popular books about time travel.

1. Mark Twain, *A Connecticut Yankee in King Arthur's Court* (1889)

2. H.G. Wells, *The Time Machine* (1895)

3. Madeleine L'Engle, *A Wrinkle in Time* (1962)

4. Jack Finney, *Time and Again* (1970)

5. Connie Willis, *The Doomsday Book* (1993)

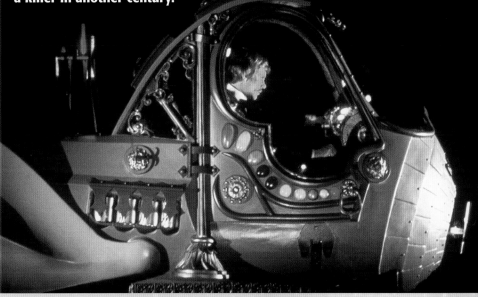

In the 1979 fantasy movie *Time After Time*, H.G. Wells, played by actor Malcolm McDowell, travels in a time machine to catch a killer in another century.

Rethink—and Discover!

Scientists are trained to keep an open mind when they do experiments. They know that the greatest discoveries are the ones that make them change their beliefs about how stuff works.

Rings in Space

Roger Penrose is a mathematician and a cosmologist, someone who studies the universe. Penrose disagrees with cosmologists who think the universe began with a "big bang" —a cosmic explosion that started from a single point in time. Instead, he believes the universe has had several cycles of big bangs. Each cycle sent out tremendous waves of energy, causing galaxies to collide. To support his theory, Penrose points to data that shows concentric "rings" around galaxy clusters. The rings, he says, are the traces of cyclical, or recurring, big-bang events. Could there be another bang in our future?

For the Record

Concentric circles have the same center. For example, imagine a large circle with a small circle inside it, and an even smaller circle inside the small one!

Do you remember reading about Penrose somewhere else in this book? Check out page 99 to find out!

Human 2.0

Charles Darwin, the English naturalist who is famous for his theory of evolution, probably wouldn't be surprised to hear that humans are still an evolving species. Geneticists, scientists who study genes, are tracking changes in the human gene pool that lead to new genetic traits and abilities. Soon, for example, fewer people may get malaria, because humans today with malaria-resistant genes are more likely to survive and have malaria-resistant kids. One scientist predicts that over the next 1,000 years, many humans will evolve into seven-foot-tall people and that a 120-year life span will be common!

An 1873 caricature of Charles Darwin, British naturalist and author of *On the Origin of Species.*

FALL 1993 $3.50

SPECIAL ISSUE
TIME

Take a good look at this woman. She was created by a computer from a mix of several races. What you see is a remarkable preview of . . .

THE NEW FACE OF AMERICA
How Immigrants Are Shaping the World's First Multicultural Society

```
0  72440 10513  3      35
```

As people from different races intermarry, the human gene pool will change. In 1993, TIME magazine imagined what a typical future American woman would look like.

BTW

According to Darwin's theory of evolution, species that adapt best to their environment are most likely to survive and reproduce. In other words: If changes in a gene are helpful to humans, a human with that gene is more likely to survive than a human without it.

CHAPTER 13

STRANGE BUT TRUE

Sites and Sights

What's the difference between site and sight? (A site is a place, a sight is something worth seeing.) But come to think of it, you can see some pretty strange sights at sites around the world. Here's a quick tour of some of the weirdest.

Strange

A Texas ranch for swanky old cars…

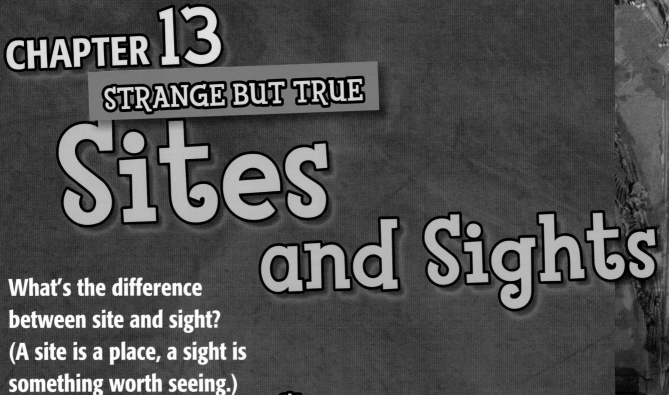

In This Chapter

- The Big Squeeze
- Puzzling Public Statues
- Wacky Celebrations
  And Much More!

Stranger
A chapel decked out with skulls and bones…

Strangest
A rock concert—with no instruments!

American Oddities

From the East Coast to the West Coast, the United States stretches about 3,000 miles. In between, there are some pretty awesome places to visit. So get out your map and plan a trip that includes these off-the-beaten-path locations!

TEXAS
Cattlelac Ranch

The state of Texas is known for its huge cattle ranches—and also for a ranch that shows off cars instead of cows. At **Cadillac Ranch**, near Amarillo, Texas, tourists can see a range of old Cadillacs that were built between 1949 and 1963 and are half-buried in the ground. This is one place where graffiti is welcome: Spraying art on the cars is a tradition that visitors honor.

FLORIDA
Eternal Youth

In St. Augustine, Florida, a freshwater spring runs through the site of an ancient Timucua Indian village. Spanish explorer **Juan Ponce de León** came here in 1513, lured by tales that drinking the water brought eternal youth. That didn't happen to de León, who died in 1521, but people still flock to the "Fountain of Youth" to sip the waters. So far, no one's gotten any younger.

Blast from the Past

When Ponce de León explored the area in 1513, it was spring, and the flowers were in full bloom. He named the place *La Florida*, which in Spanish means "Flowery Land."

This cow mural is made entirely of corncobs.

SOUTH DAKOTA

A Corny Attraction

The popcorn Americans love to munch comes from the Corn Belt in the Midwest. In 1892, the people of Mitchell, South Dakota, built a truly corny place where farmers could celebrate at harvest time. **The Corn Palace** is still standing and is decorated each year with murals made of 13 different colors of corn that show scenes of fields and farms. The Palace hosts a yearly corn festival, as well as concerts and sporting events.

It's a Wide, Weird World

Humans have traveled the world over in search of beautiful landscapes and exciting experiences. Here are some of the most bizarre destinations.

LOCATION: THE MALDIVES
Overnight Underwater

How does it feel to sleep with the fishes? Travelers who want to know can visit **King Deluxe Water Villa**, an underwater hotel in the Maldives, an island nation in the Indian Ocean. Not only can you sleep beneath the sea, you can also have breakfast, complete with schools of fish peeking through the window. Do you think fish is on the menu?

LOCATION: SWITZERLAND
A Cool Reception

Jungfrau (*yung*-frow) is only the third-highest mountain in the Bernese Alps of Switzerland, but it is home to the world's highest-altitude ice palace. Carved into the glacier by a mountaineer in the 1930s, the **Jungfrau Ice Palace** features a series of icy rooms with chairs, tables, an igloo, and sculptures of people and animals.

The Sedlec chandelier is made from every bone in the human body!

LOCATION: CZECH REPUBLIC
Watch That Clavicle!

If you have a strange sense of humor, you'll get a chuckle from a bizarre chapel in Sedlec, Czech Republic. The ossuary inside the chapel is decorated with human bones! The story goes that an old cemetery at the site was dug up when the Sedlec church was built in 1400, and the bones were moved to the chapel. More than 400 years later, a local wood-carver used them to create the decorations that today amaze, or spook, thousands of tourists.

Time to Celebrate!

No matter what corner of the world folks live in, they can always organize a festival to celebrate something they think is fun or important. But some festivals are stranger than others.

Don't Get Rattled

WHERE: Sweetwater, Texas
WHEN: Second weekend in March

There are lots of rattlesnakes in the wilds of West Texas, particularly a species called the western diamondback. There are also lots of Texans who are determined to control the diamondback population. At the yearly Rattlesnake Roundup, people try to capture as many rattlers as possible, then turn their meat into a meal and the skins into belts or boots. The biggest reptiles can be viewed at the popular Rattlesnake Exhibit. For lunch, folks munch on deep-fried rattlesnake—considered a real treat in this part of the country.

Pirates' Delight

WHERE: Lake Charles, Louisiana
WHEN: First two weekends in May

Piracy is no joke, unless you live near Lake Charles, Louisiana. The Contraband Days festival is a kooky celebration of Louisiana's most famous pirate and his crew, Jean Lafitte and the Buccaneers. The men terrorized the region in the early 19th century and may have buried their loot somewhere along the banks of the lake. One popular tradition of this all-pirate celebration is to force the mayor of Lake Charles to walk the plank. But not to worry, he's rescued when he hits the water.

Jean Lafitte

Boppin' Around

WHERE: Porto, Portugal
WHEN: June 23

One of the weirdest street fairs is held every year in Porto, Portugal. At the festival of Saint John (or *São João* in Portuguese), people arm themselves with a little plastic hammer or a large leek (a type of onion) and roam the streets bopping other people on the head—for good luck, according to tradition.

Root for the Radish

WHERE: Oaxaca, Mexico
WHEN: December 23

In most places, radishes are nothing more than colorful, peppery salad vegetables. But they are not for eating during the Night of the Radishes in Oaxaca (wa-*ha*-ka), a city in southwestern Mexico. Every year, three days before the event (called *Noche de Rábanos* in Spanish), Mexican artists start sculpting the bright red roots into animals, dancers, devils, and scenes of Oaxacan life. The artisan who creates the best radish sculpture is awarded a cash prize.

Strange Statues

Check out these strange-looking statues in cities around the world. What would you think if you happened to walk by one of them?

WHERE:
Los Angeles, California

Looks like this man in downtown Los Angeles had a really bad day at the office.

They said
I had a head
for business.
They said
to get ahead
I had to lose
my head.
They said
be concrete
& I became
concrete.
They said,
go, my son,
multiply,
divide, conquer.
I did my best.

WHERE: Turku, Finland

The Finnish artist who created this 16-foot-high pig-duck statue says he is concerned that modern gene technology will create strange new life-forms.

WHERE:
Paris, France

This statue was inspired by a French short story, "The Man Who Could Walk Through Walls." But somehow, this guy got stuck along the way.

WHERE:
Shanghai, China

Created for the Spanish pavilion at the 2010 World Expo in Shanghai, this 21-foot-tall animatronic baby, named Miguelín, "breathes" and blinks--but never needs its diaper changed. Its creator, Isabel Coixet, is seen here next to him.

The Big Squeeze

Artist Kurt Perschke is having a ball these days: a big, red, inflatable vinyl ball that he squeezes into impossible spaces around the world. He calls the traveling artwork his RedBall Project. Here is the ball in Taiwan.

BTW

RedBall is 15 feet tall and weighs 250 pounds. It's made out of the same tough material as an inflatable raft or boat. Perschke loves hearing from local citizens about the best spots in their city to place it.

For the Record

So far, RedBall has bounced around the world, squeezing into such cities as Abu Dhabi, United Arab Emirates; St. Louis, Missouri; Chicago, Illinois; and Toronto, Canada. Will it turn up in your neighborhood?

Music to the Ears

Many different items can be used to make music. Laundry equipment, thin air, and electromagnetic fields are just some of them.

Squeaky-Clean Music

Long ago, Americans used washboards to scrub their clothes. As they scrubbed, they realized that the board produced great rhythmic sounds. Soon, washboards became an instrument popular with American folk musicians, especially in Appalachia, where they're still used in jug bands today. There's even a yearly **washboard music festival in Logan, Ohio**—the town with the only remaining washboard manufacturing company in the U.S.

Rock the Air

Do you enjoy playing air guitar? Since 1996, air guitarists have been strutting their stuff in Oulu, Finland, at the **Annual Air Guitar World Championships.** The festival celebrates the art of making pretend-music. Contestants are judged on their technical merit, stage presence, and "airness"—meaning their ability to give an exciting performance.

This woman is playing a theremin. The antenna at the left stands straight up, and the horizontal one on the right curves.

Eerie Music

One of the strangest electronic instruments is the **theremin**, named after its Russian inventor, **Leon Theremin** (small photo, right), who created it in 1919. The oddest thing about it is that it's played without being touched. Instead, you wave your hands between two antennas—one vertical, one horizontal—that are each surrounded by an electromagnetic field. The movement of the hands interrupts the flow of energy in the field and produces the eerie sound you hear in old science-fiction and horror movies.

CHAPTER 14

Really
STRANGE BUT TRUE

What's the strangest thing you've learned so far? In this chapter you will find some pretty crazy stuff… and you'll be challenged to tell the strange but true from the strange and fake!

In This Chapter

- Strange Superstitions
- Portable Crosswalks
- A Fact-or-Fiction Quiz

And Much More!

Strange
A slippery way to catch the subway train…

Stranger

Alarm clocks that roll away, run on fake-hamster power, or snooze by laser gun…

Strangest

A fateful Mayan prophecy that spells DOOM! (Or does it?)

Nutty Notions

There are a lot of superstitions and ideas that some people insist are true, even when there's plenty of evidence to the contrary.

B.C. (Before Columbus!)

For hundreds of years, people have known that the Earth is round. Explorers proved this when they circled the globe instead of falling off. More recently, satellite photos of Earth taken from space clearly show its spherelike shape. But you can't convince the members of the Flat Earth Society. The international organization clings to a medieval idea: that our planet is a flat plane.

It's a Date

Some people believe the Mayan calendar (pictured) predicted the end of the world. Other "doomsday prophets" have even given an exact date, only to see the day quietly come and go. Still, many people continue to believe these gloomy predictions. Some even give away their belongings in preparation for the End of Days—and are probably very sorry the next morning!

One, Two, Three, X

Ichi, ni, san, shi, go (ee-chee, nee, sahn, she, go). That's how to count to five in Japanese. Only, the Japanese think it's unlucky to say *shi*, because the word is a homophone—a soundalike—for the word for death. So people in Japan replace *shi* with *yon* and move on to go! If you think that's a silly superstition, consider this: Many skyscrapers in the United States don't have a 13th floor!

A Peas-ful New Year

On New Year's Day in New Orleans, Louisiana, it's a tradition to eat a dish called Hoppin' John, in which the main ingredient is black-eyed peas. The superstition says that if you eat 12 black-eyed peas, one for each month of the year, you'll have good luck. Some folks think that eating a bit of collard greens brings riches too.

On the Move

There are many solutions to getting from here to there. Here are three unique examples.

For the Record

The slide's official name is "transfer accelerator"— meaning that it's a speedy way to move a passenger from street level to the station platform!

Slide and Ride

If you live in the city of Utrecht, in the Netherlands, you don't have to run for the next train—you can zip down a **slide** to reach the station!

Show Your Stripes

Crossing a busy street in Japan may require people to carry their own equipment. The creators of the **Portable Zebra Crossing** claim their invention makes it safe to cross the street where there's no crosswalk. Of course, it's dangerous to roll it out when cars are coming. And pedestrians will need to roll the mat back up once they've reached the other side.

Licensed to Chill

Lots of us enjoy an ice-cream cone on a hot summer day. Those looking to cool off on the river Thames, in London, England, can pick up a treat from the world's first **amphibious ice-cream truck**. The truck's owner decided to take to the water because noise-pollution laws have reduced the number of musical ice-cream trucks on city streets.

Sound the Alarm!

Real sleepyheads apparently need more than a simple *buzzzzzzz* or *ringgggggg* to get them up and out of bed in the morning. To help them, inventors have come up with some very unusual alarm clocks.

Flying Alarm Clock

When the alarm goes off, part of the clock takes off, helicopter-style, so you have to haul your butt out of bed to make it stop shrieking!

Laser-Target Alarm Clock

When the alarm bells ring, pick up your laser gun and aim for the target. The only way to turn off the noise is to hit the bull's-eye with the laser beam!

10 more minutes, please!

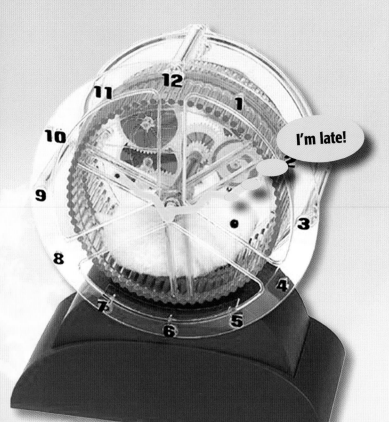

I'm late!

Hamster-Powered Alarm Clock

A fake hamster powers a wheel that moves this clock's minute hand toward wake-up time.

Runaway Alarm Clock

When you want more z's, you press the snooze button on your alarm clock. That's when Clocky really wakes up! Tell Clocky to snooze and it quietly rolls off the nightstand and out of sight. When Clocky rings again, you have to get up and hunt for the alarm to turn it off.

BTW

Clocky was invented in the media lab of the Massachusetts Institute of Technology (MIT). It has a computer inside that guides it to a new hiding place every morning!

Fact or Fiction?

Sometimes the truth is stranger than fiction. Can you tell which of these are false and which are strange but true? Answers are at the bottom of the following page.

1 The speed we sneeze at is over 100 m.p.h.

2 The official language of Cambodia, Khmer, has 74 letters in its alphabet.

3 The names of Popeye's four nephews are Pipeye, Peepeye, Pupeye, and Poopeye.

4 There are giant alligators living in the New York City sewer system.

5 About 60% of our body weight is water.

6 There are no penguins living in the North Pole.

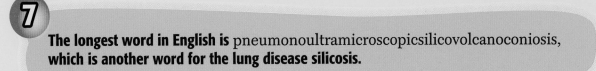

7 The longest word in English is pneumonoultramicroscopicsilicovolcanoconiosis, which is another word for the lung disease silicosis.

To be or not to be, that is the question.

8 Lightning never strikes twice in the same place.

9 A cockroach can live for weeks without its head.

10 If you touch a toad, you'll get a wart.

11 The sentence The quick brown fox jumps over the lazy dog uses every letter in the alphabet.

12 Snakes can hypnotize people by staring into their eyes.

13 If you eat nothing but carrots, your skin can turn orange.

Answers: 1. True 2. True 3. True 4. False 5. True 6. True 7. True 8. False 9. True 10. False 11. True 12. False 13. True

Index

Credits

Cover: Life on White/Getty Images (snake); Terrafugia Inc. (plane/car)

Back cover: Craig Deutsch for R studio T (pencil & girl); Tobias Nilsson (man with moustache); Alex Holden (Dalek)

2-3: Yayoi Kusama, *The Obliteration Room* 2011, installation at the Gallery of Modern Art, Brisbane. Courtesy: Ota Fine Arts, Tokyo, ©Yayoi Kusama (Obliteration Room); Michael Hewes/Getty Images (horse); Scott Barbour/Getty Images (pancake race); Fred Selby, www.watercar.com (car)

4-5: John McCormick/Virginia Tech (robot); SOM (al-Hamra); Craig Deutsch for R studio T (girl) Gregg DeGuire/FilmMagic/Getty Images (Mickey); Steve Carrasco/SixPointThree Photography (bronze statue); fixer00/shutterstock (hand); alexsvirid/shutterstock (toad); Stefano Cavoretto/shutterstock (Mayan calendar)

6-7: Craig Deutsch for R studio T (pencil); Kiselev Andrey Valerevich/shutterstock (invisible kid); Jochem D Wijnands/Getty Images (*Tomatina*); Craig Deutsch for R studio T (girls & gummy worms); Jamie Chung for TIME (cat's ears); Kerry Smith (Big merino ram); David Sacks/Getty Images (fakir)

8-9: Indraneil Das/CI/www.conservation.org (frog); Jeremy Durkin/Rex Features/AP Images (turtle); Robin Pilley (dog & toys)

10-11: Indraneil Das/CI/www.conservation.org (frog); Frank Glaw (snake); Top 5: 1: Steve Wilson/shutterstock; 2: Levent Konuk/shutterstock; 3: Flip Nicklin/Minden Pictures; 4: Laurent Fievet/AFP/Getty Images; 5: Victor Soares/shutterstock

12-13: Chris Newbert/Minden Pictures (cardinalfish); Tom McHugh (hagfish); Lander/public domain (olm); Norbert Wu/Minden Pictures (elephant fish)

14-15: Reiri Kurihara/AP Images (Ban); infinity21/shutterstock (Lhasa apso); Susan McKenzie/shutterstock (calico)

16-17: Robin Pilley (dog & toys); Mark Olinski (dog's face); Diana Mower/shutterstock (flowers); irin-k/shutterstock (bee); umbertoleporini/shutterstock (boy); Treenoot/shutterstock (pigeon)

18-19: Jeremy Durkin/Rex Features/AP Images (turtle); Jim Incledon/AP Images (cat); Paul Moseley/MCT/Newscom (Midnite)

20-21: Piotr Naskrecki/Minden Pictures (bat); Louise Emmons (chinchilla rat); Piotr Naskrecki/Minden Pictures (spider); Jessica Jeichmann (salamander)

22-23: Jon Sullivan (broccoli); Dorling Kindersley/Getty Images (cactus); Malcolm Coe/Getty Images (Hydnora); Stephen Dalton/Minden Pictures (touch-me-not)

24-25: Timothy A. Clary/AFP/Getty Images (Sir Lancelot Encore); Heidi Schumann/The New York Times (Missy Two & Mira); PPL Therapeutics/BWP Media/Getty Images (Dolly); Marco Busdraghi/Creative Commons (sea urchin) Joel Sartore/Getty Images (salamanders)

26-27: Michael Hewes/Getty Images (horse); Fabrice Coffrini/AFP/Getty Images (turtle); Alberto J. Espiñeira Francés-Alesfra/Getty Images (crane); Paul Dix/Getty Images (frog)

28-29: Inc-Photo/Getty Images (man panning gold); Mansell/Mansell/Time & Life Pictures/Getty Images (drawing); Creative Commons (map of Atlantis & Mu)

30-31: Creative Commons (map of Atlantis & Mu); Ira Block/Getty Images (gold earring); Mansell/Time & Life Pictures/Getty Images (Fawcett); David James/AP Images (Harrison Ford); Public domain (King Solomon's temple)

32-33: Pete Ryan/Getty Images (Gold Dust town); Inc-Photo/Getty Images (man panning gold); Kean Collection/Archive Photos/Getty Images (mining camp)

34-35: Extreme-Photographer/Getty Images (main photo); Joe LeMonnier for TIME FOR KIDS (maps)

36-37: Bob Thomas/Popperfoto/Getty Images (Shackleton); Colin Monteath/Getty Images (book); Universal History Archive/Getty Images (Amundsen); Public domain (poster); Mansell/Mansell/Time & Life Pictures/Getty Images (drawing); SSPL/Getty Images (medicine kit)

38-39: Carl Court/AFP/Getty Images (chess); Scott Barbour/Getty Images (pancake race); Eric L. Watts, www.trektrak.com (Klingon pageant)

40-41: Carl Court/AFP/Getty Images (chess); Creative Commons (ironing); Pedro Romero/Creative Commons (bossaball)

42-43: Raphael Gaillarde/Gamma-Rapho/Getty Images (skijoring); Tom McGann (Coney Island Polar Bear Club); Mike Timo/Getty Images (snow bikes)

44-45: ; Craig Deutsch for R studio T (girl eating jalapeño); Jochem D Wijnands/Getty Images (*Tomatina*)

46-47: Mark Scase, www.snailracing.net (snail racing); Loyal Nanaimo Bathtub Society, www.bathtubbing.com (bathtub race); Gregory Shaver/AP Images (duck derby, top); Shauna Bittle/AP Images (duck derby, bottom); Creative Crop/Getty Images (rubber duck)

48-49: Eric L. Watts, www.trektrak.com (Klingon pageant); Action Press/Rex Features (bunnies); Tobias Nilsson (moustache top & bottom small photos), Phil Olsen (moustache, large photo) both courtesy of www.worldbeardchampionships.com

50-51: Ludinko/shutterstock (LED bulb); Jamie Chung for TIME (hummingbird); U.S. Patent and Trademark Office (dimple machine); Viachaslau Kraskouski/shutterstock (boy)

52-53: Public domain (Morse code); Kesu/shutterstock (sign language); Clive Streeter/Getty Images (Marconi's transmitter); Time & Life Pictures/Getty Images (Gutenberg book); Jarod Rawsthorne/Getty Images (typewriter); Universal History Archive/Getty Images (Lumière); Nick Dolding/Getty Images (mobile phone); Luca Sage/Getty Images (iPad)

54-55: Yannik Tylle for Unicef (drum); Eric Tanner for TIME (magic mirror); Senseg (E-Sense)

56-57: U.S. Patent and Trademark Office (dimple machine & saddle); Courtesy of Fred Selby, www.watercar.com (Python); Ames Montgomery for R studio T (bar graph)

58-59: SSPL/Science Museum/Getty Images (Leonardo sketch); Peter Chadwick/Getty Images (flying machine model); Mike Stocker/Orlando Sentinel/MCT/Getty Images (jetpack); Hulton Archive/Getty Images (Jetsons)

60-61: Africa Studio/shutterstock (incandescent lightbulb); Education Images/UIG/Getty Images (Edison); Chris Hill/shutterstock (fluorescent bulb); ludinko/shutterstock (LED bulb); Lior Mizrahi/Getty Images (Dead Sea Scroll); Public domain (codex); Dmitry Lobanov/shutterstock (e-reader); Top 5: All photos Getty Images except George Caswell (landline phone)

62-63: Jamie Chung for TIME (hummingbird); David Sams/Getty Images (rat); Fraunhofer Umsicht (blades); Jens Kuhfs/Getty Images (whale); Joseph Subirana (turbine blades, center); Steve Dewar (turbine blades, right)

64-65: All images courtesy of Terrafugia Inc.

66-67: Ana Gram/shutterstock (fortune cookies); Chad Ehlers/Getty Images (subway pusher); Anthony Collins/Getty Images (Roman toilets); SuperStock/Getty Images (Roman mosaic)

68-69: Chad Ehlers/Getty Images (subway pusher); Sofia Santos/shutterstock (whistling emoticon); Ana Gram/shutterstock (fortune cookie)

70-71: Millard H Sharp/Getty Images (alligator); Lance Murphey/AP Images (tiger trainer); Martin Harvey/Getty Images (snake milker); Jonnystockphoto/shutterstock (mosquito)

72-73: Route66/shutterstock (Roman masks); DEA/G. Dagli Orti/Getty Images (scribe); Anthony Collins/Getty Images (Roman toilets); SuperStock/Getty Images (Roman mosaic)

74-75: John McCormick/Virginia Tech (robot); Jamie Chung for TIME (cat's ears); Kiselev Andrey Valerevich/shutterstock (invisible kid)

76-77: BestPhotoStudio/shutterstock (girl); Roxana Gonzalez/shutterstock (mouse); Robert Adrian Hillman/shutterstock (cryogenics); Tamara Kulikova/shutterstock (blueberry); Georges Gobet/AP Images (Calment)

78-79: Pytak/Creative Commons (Robosapien); Courtesy of Michele Guarnieri, www.hibot.co.jp (Expliner); Creative Commons (pillowbot); Hulton Archive/Getty Images (Elektro); John McCormick/Virginia Tech (robot)

80-81: Jamie Chung for TIME (all photos); Leandro Castelao for TIME (illustration)

82-83: www.mindflexgames.com (Mindflex); Kiselev Andrey Valerevich/shutterstock (invisible kid); Courtesy of Gallant Lab at UC Berkeley (movie scans)

84-85: Courtesy of Billabong.com (wet suit); Karkas/shutterstock (shirt); Albert Ziganshin/shutterstock (germ); Petrovski & Ramone/Iris van Herpen (3-D dress); Jannes Frubel (QMilch)

86-87: Leandro Castelao for TIME (PossessedHand); Jamie Chung for TIME (cat's ears); Wacom (inkling pen); Zebra Imaging (sandtable); Ben Hider/Getty Images (Watson)

88-89: Eric Ryan/Getty Images (McQueen dress); Loek van Derklis (beach sculpture); Yayoi Kusama, *The Obliteration Room* 2011, installation at the Gallery of Modern Art, Brisbane. Courtesy: Ota Fine Arts, Tokyo, ©Yayoi Kusama (Obliteration Room)

90-91: Courtesy of Ace Gallery, Los Angeles, CA (Donovan); M.C. Escher's *House of Stairs* ©2012, The M.C. Escher Company-Holland. All rights reserved. www.mcescher.com (Escher)

92-93: Loek van Derklis (all photos)

94-95: Eric Ryan/Getty Images (McQueen dress); AP Images (cream-puff dress); Matthew Peyton/Getty Images (zoot suit)

96-97: Yayoi Kusama, *The Obliteration Room* 2011, installation at the Gallery of Modern Art, Brisbane. Courtesy: Ota Fine Arts, Tokyo, ©Yayoi Kusama (all photos)

98-99: Natalie Miebach (The Perfect Dance); Alex Holden (Dalek); Bjørn Christian Tørrissen (3-D tribar)

100-101: Andy Z./shutterstock (Luxor Hotel); littleny/shutterstock (Las Vegas); Fernando Alda (Parasol); Robert Kwiatek/AFP/Getty Images (upside-down house)

102-103: Robert Kwiatek/AFP/Getty Images (upside-down house); Javier Senosiain, www.arquitecturaorganica.com (nautilus house); Trevor Johnston for TIME For Kids

104-105: Andy Z./shutterstock (Luxor Hotel); Evan Meyer/shutterstock (Hearst Castle); bbqi (Tianzi Hotel)

106-107: Fernando Alda (Parasol, small and large photo); Jürgen Mayer H. (BTW)

108-109: ©OMA (Interlace House); SOM (al-Hamra)

110-111: China Photos/Getty Images (Lunga); Donaven Staab, Santa Cruz Beach Boardwalk, www.beachboardwalk.com (Nik Wallenda); Keith Allison/Creative Commons (man in a box)

112-113: China Photos/Getty Images (Goloborodko); China Photos/Getty Images (Lunga); deepblue-photographer/shutterstock (frontbend); Public domain (backbend); Keith Allison/Creative Commons (man in a box)

114-115: All photos Craig Deutsch for R studio T except Meiko Arquillos (eyebrow raising)

116-117: Sakchai Lalit/AP Images (Spider-Men); Donaven Staab, Santa Cruz Beach Boardwalk, www.beachboardwalk.com (Nik Wallenda)

118-119: Michaela Rehle via Reuters (Nock); Public domain, Niagara Falls Public Library (Spelterini)

120-121: David Sacks/shutterstock (fakir); AFP/Getty Images (sword-swallowing festival); Keith Srakocic/AP Images (Willey)

122-123: Dirk Ercken/shutterstock (sign-carrying ant); Natalia Kolesnikova/AFP/Getty Images (ice rook); Peel Engineering (P50); Craig Deutsch for R studio T

124-125: Craig Deutsch for R studio T (pencil); Courtesy of Clemens F. Leonhardt, www.leonhardtweb.de (motorcycle); Kerry Smith (Big merino ram)

126-127: Peel Engineering (P50); Courtesy of Anatoly Konenko (aquarium); Cri-Cri Aerobatic Aircraft Building Site (Cri-Cri); AWAIBA (camera)

128-129: Jim Luzzi/Getty Images (cheese hat); Natalaia Kolesnikova/AFP/Getty Images (ice rook); Stringer/AFP/Getty Images (ice chess); Craig Deutsch for R studio T

130-131: 3drenderings/shutterstock (octopus illustration); Isantilli/shutterstock (squid ink); JelenaA/shutterstock (menu); Public domain (*ambuyat*); Marshall Astor/Creative Commons (balut)

132-133: Isantilli/shutterstock (squid ink); andrewphoto/shutterstock (blood sausage); Andre Nantel/shutterstock (fiddlehead fern); 3drenderings/shutterstock (octopus illustration); JelenaA/shutterstock (menu); Anup Shah/Getty Images (civet)

134-135: Felix Mizioznikov & Aaron Amat/shutterstock, image editing by John Gibson (chef); deepblue-photographer/shutterstock (horsemeat); pichayasri/shutterstock (shrimp); grafica/shutterstock (ice soup); Marshall Astor/Creative Commons (balut); jabiru/shutterstock (marmite); Public domain (*ambuyat*); Jorge Gobbi (guinea pig); Glenne/shutterstock (nutria illustration)

136-137: Gregg DeGuire/FilmMagic/Getty Images (Mickey); Courtesy of Peter Terren, www.tesladownunder.com (homemade Tesla coil); keko-ka/shutterstock, image editing by Ames Montgomery (old man silhouette)

138-139: Public domain (Tesla photos); Courtesy of Time Inc. (cover); Courtesy of Peter Terren, www.tesladownunder.com (homemade Tesla coil)

140-141: Gregg DeGuire/FilmMagic/Getty Images (Mickey); Asturianu/shutterstock, image editing by John Gibson; Gareth Cattermole/Getty Images (Dumbledore); Warner Bros./Getty Images (*Time After Time*)

142-143: Bob Mahoney/Time Life Pictures/Getty Images (Penrose); Science Source/Getty Images (Darwin); Courtesy of Time Inc. (cover)

144-145: Oliver Strewe/Getty Images (Cadillac Ranch); Marcin Szala/Creative Commons (Sedlec ossuary); Zona Foto, www.zonafoto.net (air guitar player)

146-147: Oliver Strewe/Getty Images (Cadillac Ranch); Anne Rippy/Getty Images (Ponce de León); S. Solum/PhotoLink/Getty Images (Corn Palace, top); Time & Life Pictures/Getty Images (Corn Palace, bottom)

148-149: Conrad Rangali Island Maldives Resort (Maldives resort); Panoramic Images/Getty Images (Jungfrau); Marcin Szala/Creative Commons (Sedlec ossuary)

150-151: Richard Ellis/Getty Images (rattlesnake roundup); Robert Frerck/Getty Images (radishes); Public domain (Lafitte); fivespots/shutterstock (rattlesnake)

152-153: Steve Carrasco/SixPointThree Photography (L.A. bronze statue); Anssi Koskinen (pig-duck); Yves Talensac/Getty Images (man through walls); Philippe Lopez/AFP/Getty Images (Miguelín)

154-155: Swanky Hsiao

156-157: Zona Foto, www.zonafoto.net (air guitar player); Courtesy of Dennis Heebink, www.washboardmusicfestival.com (washboard player); Stefan Menne/Getty Images (woman playing theremin); Topical Press Agency/Getty Images (Theremin)

158-159: HIK-ontwerpers, www.hik-ontwerpers.nl (slide); gizmodo (laser-target alarm clock); John Gibson (hamster clock); MIT Media Lab (clocky); Stefano Cavoretto/shutterstock (Mayan calendar)

160-161: Courtesy of The Flat Earth Society (T-shirt); Stefano Cavoretto/shutterstock (Mayan calendar); Pack-Shot/shutterstock, image editing by Ames Montgomery (tombstone); ZEF/shutterstock (black-eyed peas)

162-163: HIK-ontwerpers, www.hik-ontwerpers.nl (slide); japgadgets (zebra crossing); Inhabitat (ice-cream truck)

164-165: gizmodo (laser-target alarm clock); www.thinkgeek.com (flying alarm clock); John Gibson (hamster clock); MIT Media Lab (clocky); Craig Deutsch for R studio T (girl sleeping)

166-167: Blambca/shutterstock (sneezing illustration); King Features Syndicate, Inc. (Popeye's nephews); Evgenia Bolyukh (cockroach); calbers/shutterstock (lightning); fixer00/shutterstock (hand); alexsvirid/shutterstock (toad); dedMazay/shutterstock (snake); Howard Sayer/shutterstock (orange girl); Herbert Kratky/shutterstock (penguin); Rui Vale de Sousa/shutterstock (boy); Shutter Lover/shutterstock (alligator); littleny/shutterstock (subway station); ben bryant/shutterstock (Khmer text)

Maps: vector images by shutterstock, modified by R studio T, unless indicated otherwise. All backgrounds by shutterstock, unless indicated otherwise.

Crack the Code

In the world of espionage, spies often use a book cipher to swap secrets. There's no high-tech equipment needed to send and receive coded messages: Each spy needs only a copy of the exact same book—whether it's Harry Potter or Mother Goose. Put the book cipher to work! Follow the clues below to decode a special message hidden in this book.

- The first number is the page number.
- The initials correspond with the first letter of each word in one of the headlines on the page.
- The second number refers to a specific line beneath the headline.
- The third number points to a word in the line.
- The last number gives you the letter in the word.

EXAMPLE:

Here's how to find the first letter of the code:

19	MTA	4	11	3	= G
page 19	Midnite Trots Again	line 4	word 11	letter 3	=

Now it's your turn:

19	MTA	4	11	3	= G
56	TTOC	7	4	2	= O
36	AA	6	3	1	= O
154	BTW	2	3	5	= D
43	BTS	2	9	1	= J
132	VFF	1	8	1	= O
91	SINB	4	1	1	= B

139	FTR	1	2	3	= S
105	AAC	3	4	1	= T
161	APNY	6	3	5	= R
23	PD	5	1	4	= A
119	WOA	2	7	3	= N
125	TMP	4	5	7	= G
70	WW	3	3	2	= E
84	GFF	2	2	3	= R

G O O D J O B, S T R A N G E R!